THE
700
HABITS
OF HIGHLY
INEFFECTIVE
PARENTS

THE 700 HABITS OF HIGHLY INEFFECTIVE PARENTS

JONATHAN BIGGINS

VICTORY BOOKS

VICTORY BOOKS
An imprint of Melbourne University Publishing Limited
187 Grattan Street, Carlton, Victoria 3053, Australia
mup-info@unimelb.edu.au
www.mup.com.au

First published 2009
Text © Jonathan Biggins, 2009
Design and typography © Melbourne University Publishing Limited, 2009

This book is copyright. Apart from any use permitted under the *Copyright Act 1968* and subsequent amendments, no part may be reproduced, stored in a retrieval system or transmitted by any means or process whatsoever without the prior written permission of the publishers.

Every attempt has been made to locate the copyright holders for material quoted in this book. Any person or organisation that may have been overlooked or misattributed may contact the publisher.

Text design by Nada Backovic
Typeset by TypeSkill
Printed by Griffin Press, South Australia

National Library of Australia Cataloguing-in-Publication entry

Biggins, Jonathan.

The 700 habits of highly ineffective parents / Jonathan Biggins.

9780522856538 (pbk.)

Parenting—Humor.
Child rearing—Humor.

306.8740207

Dedicated to my children
(Don't say I never did anything for you)

CONTENTS

Introduction	1
1. Why Are We Doing This?	9
2. Preparing Yourselves	21
3. Preparing the Nest	31
4. Happy Birth Day	43
5. Precious Memories, or What the Ineffective Parent Thinks Is Worth Keeping	51
6. Doctors and Nurses	61
7. Bedtime	77
8. The Creative Child	87
9. Day-Care Dreaming	99
10. The Extended Family	109
11. The Inner Child	123
12. Twins and Multiples	133
13. The Top Ten	147
14. The Active Child	157

15. Indoor Fun!   173

16. Dinnertime!   183

17. The Disciplined Child   203

18. It's Your Birthday   217

19. The Learning Child   229

20. Leftovers: A Random Selection of Ineffective Habits   245

Conclusion   253

Appendix   258

INTRODUCTION

Welcome to the world of the ineffective parent, that dismal figure traditionally held responsible for all the sins, problems, hang-ups and disappointments of their ungrateful progeny. Yes, it was mums and dads just like you who created history's long line of miscreants, from Caligula to Pol Pot, from Attila the Hun to Naomi Campbell. Who created those depressed lumps trapped in dead-end suburban lives, spending thousands on therapy, ambition thwarted? It's all your fault. And we all know where to point the finger when that ghastly child throws a tantrum at the express checkout or that teenage thug coins your car and pinches the parking money out of your glove box: we blame the ineffective parents.

And so, to some extent, we should. As the poet Philip Larkin incisively wrote:

> They fuck you up, your Mum and Dad
> They may not mean to, but they do
> They fill you with the faults they had
> And add some extra, just for you.

Mind you, he was a depressive librarian so you can't blame his parents entirely; he could've independently chosen another career path that offered a few more laughs. But he does have a point.

But I doubt that many parents wilfully strive to be ineffective—oh no, it comes much more instinctively and easily than that. Our children are the sum of us and something more, yet it's as we try to shape that extra something that things often go awry. Try as we might to avoid repeating the mistakes of our own parents, we seem unable to do so. Being a parent is to witness first-hand the glacial slowness of evolution; fashionable mores aside, deep down where it matters each generation faithfully mimics the last.

But can the blame be laid entirely at the parent's door? Shakespeare, never short of a phrase, put in a word for the long-suffering primary caregivers:

> How sharper than a serpent's tooth it is
> To have a thankless child!

How true—it's comforting to know they were turning out ungrateful little bastards back in the seventeenth century as well. And how ironic to think that Shakespeare managed to grow to be as creative as he was without having Shakespeare read to him as a child—talk about gifted and talented!

Truth of the matter is, no parent is entirely responsible for what their children turn out to be. There are complex forces beyond any parent's control: genetic inheritance, peer group pressures, environmental factors, schooling, or unknown emotionally scarring experiences that only re-emerge many years down the track. And at some point, the child becomes an individual that must take responsibility for his or her own actions. (I put this at about three years of age. They can talk—surely they realise that the dog does not want or need a haircut.)

Yet this is not a book about the *truly* dysfunctional parent, or about the sad and dismal futures that await the children

Introduction

of many abusive, criminally neglectful or unloving parents. That's too dark a world to contemplate here.

No, this is a book for those of us who, having been handed the world on an Ikea plate and having prospered in an unprecedented age of peace and economic growth, *still* think we're doing an inadequate job as parents. For those of us who jump at the slightest cough from baby, thermometer in one hand and telephone in the other, finger poised on the doctor's surgery speed dial. Those who cover the fridge with the scrawled masterpieces of our toddlers to encourage their artistic genius and tell the world about it: 'Come on, did you draw even three fingers on a hand when you were two? That is unbelievable talent!' Those who lie awake at night, fretting that they didn't inculcate their eight-year-old with enough self-esteem that day or anticipating disaster if anyone has undocumented nut allergies at the Bollywood-themed birthday party for Skiye's tenth.

Who invented the verb 'to parent' anyway? When did we stop simply having, then bringing up, kids, and start subscribing to this burgeoning 'parenting' industry? When did it stop being enough to shelter, feed, educate and love your child as best you could? In hindsight, our parents (and their parents) seemed to do a far better job with far fewer resources. And they had other things to worry about, like various world wars, the Great Depression, infant mortality, painful dentistry and no access to online gaming.

And before I stand accused of the rosy glow of nostalgia, I will admit that great strides have been made in child health, social justice, children's rights and the toy industry—some of the stuff is fantastic! Much better than the crap we had. Yet I believe we are at one of those moments where the pendulum has swung too far, a point in history where children have been brought so far to the forefront of our lives that we have lost sight of our own lives as adults in the process. And, ironically, are consequently doing our children a disservice.

Like so many aspects of modern life, child-raising became more complicated when the publishing industry got involved. You can almost track the generational differences by the parenting self-help bible that was dogma at the time—there goes a Dr Spock baby, here comes a Penelope Leach child with high self-esteem that's never had a decent clip round the earhole, there's a Robin Barker infant eating pureed greens and self–toilet training. Admittedly, there was a vacuum in the market—no-one hands you an instruction manual for this strange and foreign bundle that is now your sole responsibility when you leave the hospital, birthing centre, wading pool or whatever. Each new book promised a common-sense, no-nonsense approach to child-raising, covering everything from nappy rash to stranger danger. Each utilised the best research of the time and each contained many relevant and useful truisms. Equally, some of it was wide of the mark—Dr Spock's suggestion that babies never be laid to sleep on their backs has since been discredited as a possible contributor to sudden infant death syndrome (SIDS).

The fact is, the raising of young is a complicated, baffling, lifelong process that contains no definitive answers. While we're in the mood for quotations, let's hear from Bill Cosby, who played a father on TV and naturally was elevated in the popular press to an authority on the subject:

Introduction

> In spite of the six thousand manuals on child-raising in the bookstores, child-raising is still a dark continent and no-one really knows anything. You just need a lot of love and a lot of luck—and, of course, courage.

Other animal species seem to manage alright without professional help—have you ever seen a chimpanzee reading a child-raising book by Kaz Cooke? I am not suggesting that eating the lice out of your young's hair or encouraging them to throw faeces at zoo-goers are signs of adequate parenting skills, but do remember this: being a parent is a matter of trial and error. There's an awful lot of error and the whole thing is a trial.

So, what's the point of this book? For a start, it primarily addresses the early years, those happy days when you're still in a state of catatonic shock. This is a book written from personal experience; my children at the time of writing are nine years old—mind you, they could be twenty by the time I've finished. I only have vicarious experience of the teenage years through various nephews and nieces so best if I stick to what I know. But as more is discovered about the way a child's brain forms and the Jesuit motto of 'Give me the child until he is seven and I will give you the man' is proving increasingly prescient, it's not a bad idea to examine parenting in that crucial phase of the early years.

You can use this book in a number of ways. First, as a weapon of last resort when your children have you cornered in the rumpus room. Sadly, it's not available in hardback, but keep a few copies of *War and Peace* strategically scattered around the house—there's nothing like a well-aimed tome to the back of the head to stop them dead in their tracks. Alternatively, you can use it to prop up one end of the cheap cot you bought on eBay that is mysteriously missing one castor. Or you can dip into it when you have five minutes of peace, although you probably won't get that for quite some time.

The astute reader may notice that the book is not strictly chronological. A curious consequence of having a child is that you're only truly aware of them as they exist in the present moment. I remember berating my mother for not knowing what to do with a newborn—she'd forgotten all about it and even now, I must confess, almost everything about them has gone from my memory as well. Honestly, if you didn't have photos you wouldn't have a clue what your kids looked like when they were young. God knows what people did before the camera—asked someone in every six months to paint the kids, I dare say. So certain instructional sections of the book are generalised, rather than age specific. You may also notice that some observations are not always based on scientific truths supported by empirical evidence. They are there to demonstrate the ineffective parent's tendency to generalise.

But most importantly, I hope this book will help you to realise that you're not alone when you lose it and think your children are greedy little shits who've completely ruined your life. (Oh come on, doesn't everyone feel like that every now and then?) Or to discover that you will always be totally unprepared for the overwhelming, almost visceral feeling of love they are capable of inspiring in you. Usually when they're asleep.

Introduction

You will make so many mistakes as a parent you'll lose count. This book lists them numerically, in no particular order, and to be honest we may not get to the full 700 because … *I have not stopped, if it's not one thing it's another and when am I going to find the time to drive them to stupid bloody soccer, why can't they just play online chess, surely that's a sport, or just go for a walk for Christ's sake!!*

No, no. I'll be fine. There's a bottle of sauvignon blanc on express chill in the freezer—better still, Scotch is made with barley and that counts as a vegetable. And surely it's cocktail hour somewhere in the world.

I forgot to write anything on this page.

1

WHY ARE WE DOING THIS?

'Children begin by loving their parents; after a time they judge them; rarely, if ever, do they forgive them.'
Oscar Wilde

This page is a list of the qualifications you have to be a parent.

Have you ever stopped to wonder why you want—or wanted—to have children? To be brutally honest, the world doesn't need another single human being. The best thing you could do for the planet would be to not have any children at all and then, ideally, to top yourself.

'But my child might discover the cure for cancer!' you reply. Yes, but equally, in twenty years' time he or she could be living on the dole in a Toyota HiAce with three kids under the age of four. From an ecological point of view, there are no pressing reasons for mankind to continue to breed as rapidly and successfully as we have. But like all animals on the planet, we have this innate desire to procreate, although I suspect for a lot of us the desire has much more to do with the initial, interesting part of the process than the results.

However, unlike other animals, humans in developed societies can now make a conscious decision *not* to have children. You won't hear a gazelle saying: 'I'm happy with my lifestyle choice—the grass-eating is going well, I'm in good shape and I like my udder the way it is; I'm not going to bother with kids'. (Although, strictly speaking, a gazelle doesn't have kids, she has fawns. A goat, however, does have kids.) And many people do make that choice and lead contented and fulfilled lives. Then there are others who can't have children, despite the advances made in fertility treatments; others make choices based on sexual orientation. Which is all very well and good for them as they swan about the world with all that extra disposable income—someone has to go to the trouble of making gay people and then awkwardly marching in the Mardi Gras parade with a banner saying 'Proud Parent'. I think we should charge a fee.

11 Having children in the first place

Children were once either a blessing or a curse; another pair of helping hands on the farm or aboard the fishing boat, or another mouth to feed when already there wasn't enough mashed oats, or whatever it was they ate, to go around. In today's Western cultures, children no longer represent that sort of life-or-death decision. In fact, they've almost become an indulgence. Consequently, it's been assumed that children now serve another function, that of bringing fulfilment and purpose to life; it's believed that parents are in some way happier for the experience of raising a family. And there's no denying that children, while being frustrating, are endlessly rewarding. *I have to believe that!*

But recent research has found that there is no discernible difference in the happiness quotient between the parents and the childless. Professor Robin Simon of Florida State University has analysed the data from several large American studies and in July 2008 she was quoted in *Newsweek* as saying:

Why Are We Doing This?

> Parents experience lower levels of emotional well-being, less frequent positive emotions and more frequent negative emotions than their childless peers ... in fact, no group of parents—married, single, step or even empty-nesters—reported significantly greater emotional well-being than people who never had children.

Other studies show that happiness levels within marriages dip dramatically when the children arrive and don't resume their earlier levels until well after the children have left home. Now, of course it's impossible to quantify the heights of a 'positive emotion' or indeed the depths of the 'more frequent negative emotions'. One could argue that parents live more intense emotional lives, and isn't that what life is all about? Well, yes and no.

And if having children isn't depressing enough, wait until you find out what it's going to cost. In 2005, Dr Paul Henman of the University of Queensland concluded that the average cost of raising a child to the age of eighteen is between $120,000 and $600,000, depending on your disposable income. The average cost of raising two children is about $450,000. In other words, you can afford to fly first class around the world every year for eighteen years if you take sensible precautions in the bedroom.

However, those alarming figures have since been disputed. Associate Professor Michael Dockery of Curtin University of Technology compared over 3000 couples with and without children and found that the average wealth (housing, shares, superannuation and savings) of the two groups varied very little, leading him to conclude that the average child 'cost' about $1300 a year. God knows what the child ate and if it ever went out the front door—$1300 would hardly cover a year's lemonade, DVD hire and Smiggle stationery.

The discrepancy arises from the fact that the childless people expend more of their wealth in discretionary spending. In other words, childless couples squander their money on themselves—and why the hell wouldn't you?

12 Having children accidentally

One can understand this happening in the hot throes of first love, but for those already with children, in this day and age of reliable contraception, how is it possible? Do men inadvertently fall on their fecund wives and accidentally impregnate them? And with sexual relations being such a rare event in the post-children world, surely it can't be that hard to take precautions. You've only got to be thinking on birthdays and Christmas.

But we must note that there is a difference between the accidental and the unwanted pregnancy. The accidental, particularly in families with existing children, is often met with a resigned 'Oh well, here we go again' or a sly smile and manly cries of 'There's life in the old dog yet, eh?' And then the husband chips in with an equally amusing quip as well. On the other hand, the unwanted pregnancy is a difficult and trying time for all concerned and must be dealt with by each according to their conscience without any judgement or interference from those whose business it is none of.

13 Having children late in life

A challenge in so many ways: the lack of energy and patience, the complete destruction of your established and comfortable lifestyle, greater sleep dependence, higher career demands and grandparents who are too old for any serious grandchild minding. Despite this, the average age of women having their first pregnancy is rising, as indeed is the average age of the first-time father. Many women now choose to pursue career first and postpone starting a family, only to find, when they finally turn the biological clock off snooze, that it's not as easy as they were led to believe. Unfortunately, despite all its inherent logic and justice, feminism has been unable to alter inconvenient and unavoidable truths about the human reproductive system.

For a start, women still have to have the babies. (Well, apart from that strange person in the USA who, having undergone sex-change procedures to become a man, became pregnant. Obviously, some of the procedures had a way to go.) A fertile woman in the twenty to twenty-four age bracket has an 86 per cent chance of falling pregnant. Between thirty and thirty-five, that figure drops to 50 or 60 per cent—at age forty, she has a 36 per cent chance. Furthermore, 20 per cent of women between the ages of thirty-five and thirty-nine are infertile. The chances of diabetes, high blood pressure, pre-eclampsia and birth defects all rise as women age. And men's fertility also fades as they get older; spermatozoa, like everything else, tire more easily.

Enter the panacea of IVF treatment: the answer for some, a bitter disappointment for many. Success rates in IVF are difficult to measure and are manipulated by various interest groups to serve their own purposes, but as a general idea, it's estimated that the success rate is 17 per cent per treatment cycle. Not fabulous odds. IVF has also led to a surge in the number of twin births—one in four successful IVF procedures will deliver twins. (See the Twins and Multiples chapter.)

So think carefully before leaving your tilt at it too late. On the other hand …

14   Having children too early in life

There are programs in some high schools that allow young mothers to continue their studies, despite the fact that there were certain lessons, particularly those in what I believe is now called personal development, they patently failed to learn. Being up the duff as a teenager is probably not the best of all possible worlds. Having said that, there are some teenage relationships that blossom, despite the early arrival of children—and what better fortieth birthday present could you have than the youngest of your four children starting university?

On the plus side, you have energy, need less sleep, have fewer career demands (McDonald's offers quite flexible work hours) and there's every chance your skincare products won't be out of date by the time your child also needs to tackle unsightly spots head-on.

On the downside, you've got almost no money, little world experience, nowhere to live except with your parents and there's a lack of vocational childcare in the fast-food industry.

15   Having children to ensure your vicarious immortality

There is something nice about continuing a family tree, no matter how diseased or straggly it may have become over time. (Although honestly, for some family trees a good dose of Zero weedkiller would be a merciful release.) But don't view any future children as your passport to immortality. Who knows what could happen in the interim—they might be hit by a bus or become neo-Nazis. No, if you want a legacy that weathers the ages, you can't rely on your offspring, let alone theirs. Pursue the arts—paint something other than your living room; write an extremely good novel; record the definitive album of your generation or auteur a film that combines exquisite storytelling *and* box-office appeal. Better still, go out and win a few wars—look how famous Julius Caesar is even now.

16   Having children to compensate for your own failures

It's not a good idea to wish your kids could be everything that you weren't. If you couldn't be a ballet dancer because you were too tall, talentless and lacked the necessary drive, chances are they'll carry all those burdens as well. It's called genetics: losers breed losers—don't blame me, it's science. Ditto sporting talent. If you didn't play for Manchester United, your son probably won't either, despite having the unusual first name of Beckham.

However, should your inadequacies miraculously skip a generation, nothing will kill a child's eagerness more quickly than a parent's over-enthusiasm. Apart from those awkward teenage years when a child would rather eat its own foot than do anything actively endorsed by its parents, any child eventually resents too much encouragement. The children of pushy parents are invariably pushed over the edge.

17 Having children to please your parents

There are many pressures on people to have children: social obligation, peer expectations—even the government is getting in on the act with baby bonuses and tax rebates, imploring us to go out and make babies for the good of the country. But nothing can beat the pressure from potential grandparents. If they're that keen and endlessly nagging you to produce, take advantage of your unique bargaining power. Get something in writing, for example: they'll pay for the nursery furniture, a bigger car, provide three meals a week and guarantee seventy-eight babysits per annum.

18 Having children to get the welfare payments

According to talkback-radio hosts, this sort of thing is being done all the time. Surely it's an urban myth. Who'd be that stupid? To make any serious money, you'd have to have at least seven kids and live in a caravan. Financially, it'd be a much smarter move to sell the children because you get a big cash lump sum up front and no ongoings.

19 Having a child as a fashion statement or accessory

It does happen, with some misguided fools wanting to emulate the Hollywood A-listers, but remember that, unlike a pair of flares or a bubble skirt, you can't leave a child at the local charity op shop when they go out of fashion. They're like a tattoo: for life. So choose carefully or, if you adopt from overseas, try to work in some sort of exchange clause or limited guarantee.

20 Having children to keep a relationship together

As good ideas go, this is up there with smoking. If a relationship is in trouble, having a child is only going to accelerate the decline. By all means press ahead if the thought of being a single parent is attractive. On the plus side, going solo means the welfare payments (see habit 18) are bigger.

21 Having a relationship only to have a child

Touchy subject, but we all know of women who have seemingly formed a relationship with the sole motive of having a child. Some may call it entrapment, but let ye not judge, etc. And I dare say there have been men doing the very same thing—look at Henry VIII. However, think carefully before embarking on such a course of action. There are alternatives, such as friendly gay men, banks of a particular nature and turkey basters. Or if you're extremely desperate, I can always send something through the express post.

22 Having children because you feel you should

It is true that most of us feel at some stage in life a vague need to have children. A bit like thinking one should really see the Grand Canyon or do yoga. Being a natural psychological urge, it's as good a reason as any and I suspect that many children arrived on the planet simply because two people said: 'Why not?' For them, being a parent is essentially coping with the consequences of that decision; it's the morning after that lasts a lifetime.

Still—what else are you going to do?

This page is an illustration of the mind of a parent of four-week-old twins.

2

PREPARING YOURSELVES

'To beget children, nothing better; to have them, what iniquity!'
Jean-Paul Sartre

This page is an illustration of the mind of a parent of four-year-old twins.

So let's assume you've decided to go ahead and do it. As I mentioned earlier, nothing can *truly* prepare you for parenthood, but there are a few strategies you can adopt in readiness for that stomach-lurching moment when the nurse hands the child over with a firm 'Goodbye'. Especially if you've tried to stay in the hospital for a few extra weeks. (Herbal home-birth types can smugly ignore that last comment—in fact, most of this book, because in my experience you're largely a humourless bunch.)

Up to that point in your life, you've never been solely responsible for anything of irreplaceable value. This is bigger than not backing up your iPhoto library or borrowing your parents' car. So a certain amount of prenatal education is probably a good idea, even if most of it flies out of your head at the first real emergency, that moment when you reluctantly peer at a steaming heap that's just been expelled and exclaim: 'Oh my God, is it meant to be that colour?'.

There is a wide range of help available for prospective parents beyond the groaning shelves of the family section in the bookshop. Local childhood health centres, your GP, the maternity hospital, friends and family are all keen to pass on the secret parent business of the tribe. At times the advice can become overwhelming and ultimately you find yourself relying on instinct, which is probably why you'll make so many mistakes. And be wary of the industry that has grown up around this most essential and basic of human activities. Like everything else, birth has become an opportunity for pundits, experts, charlatans, salesmen and snake oil merchants to muscle in on. If you can't beat them, join them—so read on.

23 Thinking that your life won't really change all that much

There are those who think that life is not going to be very different after they have a child—they'll still be able to go to restaurants, work from home or attend three-day rock festivals. These people are delusional. Every aspect of your life after childbirth will be different, from your sleeping habits to when and where you eat your meals. Work will become increasingly attractive—nine hours a day at the office will seem like a holiday compared to staying at home. Forget any notion of actually working from home, baby quietly asleep in the bassinet beside the PC. For something that only weighs a few kilos, they're overwhelmingly demanding of your time and attention—they don't know you've got a deadline in two days and nothing on paper.

On the social scene, you'll discover that many of your old friends without children will not be so keen to visit. Going out becomes a trial—popping in to the local trattoria with a baby capsule and three packets of wet-wipes is usually an experience not repeated. Ditto the local cinema's mums-and-bubs matinee screening with the volume pumped up to the pain threshold in a vain attempt to cut through the incessant infant wailing.

24 Telling people the happy news

Obviously you want to share the joy, but might I counsel caution—maybe wait until the pregnancy is well established before you send out the group email. Sadly, one in four pregnancies end in miscarriage and, should it happen to you, the last thing you need to compound the emotional distress is having to let everyone know what is now the unhappy news. Thankfully, there are many support groups for those who miscarry; don't underestimate the impact it can have.

25 Not taking it easy during pregnancy

Ideally, you should rest, de-stress and take it easy when expecting a child—I know it worked for me, but I'm going to go out on a limb here and suggest that mums should try it too. Don't work too hard—does anyone say on their deathbed: 'I wish I'd spent more time at the office', apart from people who are killed on their days off? If you need to have a job, perhaps you could consider switching to one that involved sitting down a lot—interpreting at the UN, newsreading or being a telephonist in a non-automated exchange.

26 Acting as if you're the first person in the world to have a baby

That honour goes to Eve, but she didn't have anyone to brag about it to apart from Adam and a few uninterested apes, jealous of the fact that they hadn't climbed the most recent rung of the evolutionary ladder. And the missing link was at that stage already missing. It's understandable that you will feel elation, pride, excitement, nervous anticipation and an overwhelming sense of being special. Get over it, because no-one else is as remotely interested as you are. It's like a stand-up comedian who immediately devotes all her material to motherhood the moment she drops one—you knew it was coming the minute she broke the baby-bump news to *Woman's Day*, but it doesn't make it any less tedious.

27 Being a celebrity mom

They can't even spell the word correctly! If you are a genuine celebrity you might be excused from this one, but I don't understand how anyone can regard as noteworthy the pregnancy, surrogate or otherwise, of someone who considers an appearance in *Who* magazine a positive career move.

28 Not attending prenatal classes

Some people think they can go it alone, that they don't need to subscribe to a patriarchal, dehumanising health system prescribing agendas that subvert childbirth from a natural act into, like, a medical procedure, man. They believe they can get there with instinct and instructional websites like stretchyourperineumnaturally.com. Others may not be so confident, and prenatal classes can be a useful way to learn about first-time pregnancy, childbirth and the first weeks of caring for a newborn. Obviously, with subsequent births you wouldn't bother because by that stage you think you know it all.

Invariably run by either jolly or hard-bitten midwives, pre-natal classes (I hope memory serves) largely consist of sitting about on beanbags and watching graphic videos that will haunt you for months. Occasionally latex dummies are introduced to illustrate various anatomical features, birth plans are discussed, potential problems flagged and 'war stories' swapped among the nervous prospective parents. The prospective mother—who, let's face it, has to do all the work—is taught how to breathe in a pattern that, if she has any sense, allows her to grunt 'Drugs … now … drugs … now' in a rhythmic fashion. I'm still at a loss to understand why pain relief during labour is frowned upon in some circles as being unnatural. By the same logic, we would have teeth pulled without anaesthetic or leave them in situ to rot as nature intended. Perhaps if women ran the Royal College of Obstetrics, advances in painless childbirth would have progressed more rapidly. And hats off if you can pop a baby out in ten minutes, comforted only by the smell of freesias, but don't presume to lecture others for surrendering to a good old patriarchal epidural.

29 Attending prenatal classes

Contradictory advice, I know, but you might as well get used to that if you're going to be a parent. The birth of a first child and the following months all go by in such dazed confusion that anything you dutifully learned in prenatal classes flies out the window at the first contraction. As a group, you bond with your prenatal classmates, but it's a bit like being on a ship: you swap addresses, but no-one keeps in touch. Brought together by this most unifying of human experiences, you quickly realise that not much else is going to keep you together in the same room after the big day. We quickly severed ties with one couple in particular, just after they videotaped their child's first explosive bowel movement and were keen to share.

30 Talking to your child in the womb

This has been all the rage for a while now—experts, like the child-rearing author Elizabeth Noble, suggest that you talk to your unborn child and explain that they must be kind and learn to love, share and get along. You might as well explain it to the cat. Tests suggest that in-utero babies can tell the difference between light and dark, but that's way short of the complexities of a system of morality; the concept of sharing is one that escapes the well-developed mind, let alone that of someone bobbing about in an amniotic sac incapable of breathing. Ditto learning to count in the womb by tapping, appreciating Debussy, and calculus.

31 Changing your will

What's the rush? No-one wants to inherit your crippling debts, and such a dubious legacy can be a useful bargaining chip in later life.

32 Determining the sex of your child

How boring is that? Unless of course you're doing it in some mystical way like swinging a needle over the belly or observing the phases of Venus during the second trimester; that at least has some hippie value and can keep the cynics amused. But to apply the cold logic of science and deny yourself the anticipatory thrill of that first glimpse of the defining bits seems utilitarian. Life is all chance anyway and that initial fifty-fifty each-way bet is one of humanity's great joys. Obviously, if a few extra months on the waiting list of an exclusive single-sex school is useful to you, I'm afraid you're a dull and lifeless waste of space.

33 Pre-naming your child

This can be done even if you don't know the sex of your child—in fact, there are books devoted to the subject. How has choosing a name for a kid become so difficult? How has it become so time-consuming? By all means prepare a short list of possible names. I suggest you keep it down to a hundred for each sex, possibly with some cross-gender alternatives in there, just to give them options later in life; for example: Terry/Terri or Robin/Robyn (although come to think of it, when was a boy last named Robin except in the Batman comics?).

However, don't choose the name until you've seen the baby. There's every chance she won't look like a Samantha or a Britney—even less that she'll look like a Zac or an Oscar.

And don't fall victim to the alarming trend to spell names in a new and unique way, the logic being that an unusually spelt name will give your child individuality. More often than not, it simply condemns them to a lifetime of having to laboriously spell out their name every time they're asked to provide it. If, however, you do insist on giving your child a name that reads like an SMS text message, I've provided some spelling variations on a few popular names to make it easier.

THE 700 HABITS OF HIGHLY INEFFECTIVE PARENTS

TABLE 1

Madeleine	Britney	Lisa-Marie
Madeliene	Brittney	Leesa-Marie
Madelyne	Britnie	Lisa-Maree
Maddeleine	Brittiney	Lisamarie
Maddaleine	Britiny	Leeza-Marie
Maddalyne	Britainie	Lisa-Mahree
Madalign	Britainy	Lisa-Marey
Madeline	Britknee	Lise-Mari
Madaleine	Britnee	Lisamarie
Madelyne	Brytney	Leesamaree
Madelayne	Brittnie	Lees-Amarie
Madylyne	Britt-nee	Lisah-Mahrie
Madalyn	Brittany	Lisa-maree
Maddie	Brittanie	Lesa-marey
Maddy	Brithanee (the 'h' is silent)	Leesa-Maree
Maddey	Britneyh (likewise)	Llisa-Mmarie
Maeddy		Lease-a-Marie
Maddi		
Madds		
Madd (uncommon)		

Jack	Marmaduke	Caitlin
Jak	Marmeduke	Caitlyn
Jack	Marmadyuke	Caytlin
Jac	Victim	Caytlyn
Djak		Caitlynne
Jakk		Kaitlin
Jacque		Kaytlin
Jacq		Kaytlyn
Gack		Kay-t'lyn
Jaack		Kaytln
Jaak		C8lin

3

PREPARING THE NEST

'The best thing we can do is to make wherever we're lost in
Look as much like home as we can'
Christopher Fry

Use this page to map out your social calendar for the next five years.

Like the proverbial bird, many prospective parents feel a strong instinctive urge to prepare a nest for the new arrival. I think we can safely say without being accused of sexism that the fathers are perhaps somewhat less enthusiastic about this aspect of preparing for a new life. Indeed, some may be unable to distinguish this surge of home improvement and compulsive shopping from any other day of the year, while others may join in with a flurry of repainting and multiple excursions to Target with either equal enthusiasm or an air of resignation bordering on martyrdom. Clearly, a new addition to the family is going to mean some changes in the living arrangements, but careful planning is needed to avoid the pitfalls.

34 Renovating the house after seeing the first ultrasound

Obvious, one would've thought, but you'd be surprised at the number of complete idiots who begin renovations during pregnancy—we did. In our defence, we had begun the process long before the happy news; getting plans through council is a long and arduous process, just like trying to start a family except that you have to sleep with more than one person and often you don't know their first names. And once we'd been given the green light by the planning department all those years later, and the builder's window of opportunity opened just a fraction, we decided to seize the moment.

And of course, we're not talking about knocking out a wall and installing a few shelves, no, this was the complete roof-off, floor-up job, the sort of ambitious project that had the builder advising it'd be easier to simply pull the old house down and start again. But the period charm! And of course, it was twins on the way, with the builder growing more and more alarmed each time the rapidly swelling Mrs B turned up for a site inspection. Towards the end he was all but blow-drying the concrete to make it cure more quickly.

Typically, we had forgotten the first two rules of any renovation: it's going to be two months late and 20 per cent over budget. So all that money we'd set aside for the nappy service was out the window. And perversely, the twins arrived five weeks early, roughly about the same time as the plumber. Thank God for neonatal hospitalisation! They had a roof over their heads, even if it was in semi-intensive care.

So the lesson is clear: renovate, then procreate.

35 Believing you have to renovate at all

It's extraordinary how much more space we feel we need these days. Houses are now built to within a centimetre of the boundary line; inner-city worker's cottages are expanded with Tardis-like ingenuity. In the two-bedroom house across the street from us—well, two bedrooms no longer, now it's 3brs, poss 4th/study/media rm, 2.5 bth, off-str park—a family of five children was happily raised. Not sure if the kids still sleep together in the same beds even now, but the point is, don't automatically assume that baby needs its own room with ensuite just yet. It'll probably spend most of its time within arm's reach of you anyway. And don't even think about constructing a playroom. There is nothing sadder than the sight of a beautifully laid out playroom, cushions invitingly placed, educational toys on the shelves alongside the deluxe Beatrix Potter collection, colourful alphabet mural on the wall, the whole thing completely devoid of children because all they want is to play with a cardboard box and eat sand directly beneath your feet in any part of the house other than the playroom. They might be coaxed into it if you sit in there as well, but then what's the point?

Besides, there's a lot to be said for the theory of only renovating your house after the children have all but destroyed it. I know they need to be taught a sense of responsibility for their immediate environment, to learn how to care for and maintain material possessions, but frankly, that kind of rational thought process doesn't biologically kick in for many years. Usually when you threaten to ruin some item they hold dear if they don't stop writing with texta on the lounge suite. Infantile scrawling you can forgive, but HSC study notes scribbled on the Moran three piece are not on.

So best advice is live with what you've got, buy a few bunk beds later on and hold off on the all-white colour scheme for twenty years.

36 Moving house before the baby arrives

It's said that moving house can be one of the most stressful things you can do in your life. I'd have thought being shot at or watching *Australia's Got Talent* would rate more highly as stressful activities, but moving house is certainly not something you should be contemplating. Perhaps you could make an exception if you're living in a tent or dumpster but otherwise, think carefully before you make the move. Babies in their first year require a lot less space than you'd think. The paraphernalia that usually comes with them requires a storage container, but apart from that they're quite a compact unit.

37 Moving house after the baby arrives

Again, not advisable, although not as tricky as during pregnancy. Compared to the stress of the first six months of a new life, buying a house is a doddle. Do it before the child becomes too attached to their surroundings, certainly before they start school. It's amazing how fiercely a child will resist the idea of moving, even within the same neighbourhood. If you have to, try to make the move an upgrade in their eyes—a swimming pool, their own room, a small pony, that sort of thing.

38 Investing too much effort in the nursery

Preparing a nursery is tricky. Just as with the delicate timing required before informing the world at large that you're expecting, you don't want to start too early because that could be tempting fate. On the other hand, leave it too late and baby might be sleeping on the last piece of foam available in the only Clark Rubber store still open on the way home from the hospital. Most ineffective parents of a firstborn, however, make the mistake of going completely over the top with the nursery and end up doing one (or possibly two) of the following:

39   Going for the pioneer look

You know the sort of thing—scrubbed wooden floors, stained-pine change table with turned legs, rustic bassinet with mosquito net suspended from an elaborate davit, framed family photos, fresh towelettes neatly folded (possibly on a luggage rack from an old railway carriage), brass lamps, Jemima Puddleduck frieze on the wainscot and a rocking chair for those tender mother-child feeding moments as the sun gently sets, or for some Dad bonding time in the early hours. Strangely, the only time either of you sits on it is in the furniture store before you buy it.

40   Going Scandinavian

Allen keys (choking hazard!) safely packed away, this assembled flat-pack nursery looks like the Norwegian tundra during a snowstorm, with barely discernible furniture items struggling to emerge from the blinding whiteness of it all. A cot called Tjörk, a change table of brutal minimalism named Knärsten, Blinte shelves receding into the middle distance, some circular rugs of unknown material woven in the Congo scattered on the floor and a large pile of muslin squares stacked on the Bunte—whatever that is.

41   Going funky

MP3 player dock for soothing chill music, Calder mobile dangling above the Bauhaus-inspired change surface, cot that requires an engineering degree to work out how to lower the side, CCTV monitor and baby-alert wirelessly routed to the iPhone, 'how to count to ten in binary' mural on the ceiling, organic cloth nappies, poster-sized black-and-white photo-portrait of baby on father's shoulder on the wall and plenty of mirrors so the baby (although 'baby' is such a patronising word, perhaps 'potential adult' is better, although 'better' implies a qualitative judgement—I'll get back to you) can have plenty of reassuring glimpses of the self.

42 Going for the Nickelodeon look

Littlest Mermaid cot from the Target Deluxe range, Disney Pooh change table (ironic name for a change table, huh?), Bob the Builder playtime rug, Sponge Bob Square Pants beanbag, cable-wired LCD on the wall—more for Mum really, or Dad, we're doing bottles—complete Fisher Price 0–3 activity sets bought as a job lot on eBay and stacked in the built-ins, two crates of Huggies Infant nappies and an electronic Air Wick dispenser next to the night light.

43 Going for no look

Cot recommended by *Choice* magazine in an off-brown colour (only one available in metropolitan area), nappy bucket for the six weeks of paid nappy service that everyone at work clubbed together to buy, that chair from the lounge room that was always too big and realistically still is, mobile chopping block from the kitchen as a change table (didn't really use it, only got in the way and the onion smell is almost completely gone), some towels with the edges frayed, a bottle of Spray'n'Wipe and two flannels.

All are equally valid and all are equally pointless, depending on your point of view. Anyway, they're only going to be there for a few years because the next pregnancy test only shows positive the day after you've sold the lot for 10 per cent of what you paid.

44 Having an inadequate supply of towels

Even cloth squares will do, but you can never have enough towels. Babies produce an inordinate amount of fluid—they are the perfect demonstration that the body is 90 per cent liquid, and large amounts regularly discharge from various apertures. If you try cloth nappies for a few weeks and then abandon them for the nightmare that they are, keep a few handy for spills. When baby is still breast- or bottle feeding, fashion a poncho out of nappies and wear it whenever the baby is awake because you will inevitably be thrown up on at least twice a day. Polished boards or concrete are ideal floor surfaces, but anything else that can be hosed down and disinfected is equally fine.

45 Having an inadequate bathroom cabinet

Chaps, I'm afraid the men's cosmetics and skincare products are going to have to be boxed and put away to make room for baby's requirements—not that you're going to need them again anyway; your metrosexual days are well and truly over. In their place will arrive a plethora of ointments, powders, unguents and oils. All equally ineffective, but when you're confronted by a screaming infant with chafed buttocks you'll try anything. Go to the chemist and buy as much Junior Panadol as you can with a two-year expiry limit;

it's cheaper in bulk and you'll get through it, even if the baby doesn't.

46 Buying a playpen

The playpen is an excellent concept on paper, but it rarely works in the real world. No-one likes to be put in a cage, so why assume your child does? And anyway, unless you bolt it to the floor, any half-decent crawler can push the thing wherever it wants to go—next to the open flame of the heater, to the edge of the stairs, or up to the shops for a Mars bar. Some parents adopt a reverse playpen strategy; they sit in the playpen with *New Idea* and a cup of tea and let the children have the run of the house.

47 Not investing in childproof gates

Unlike the playpen, the childproof gate or interior fence is a terrific idea, particularly if you have stairs or want to keep the children out of the kitchen with all its dangerous attractions like knives and blenders. Make sure there is an opening mechanism for adults because you'll soon tire of heaving your leg over. Mind you, you're not going to get your leg over anywhere else for some time. (See habit 237, 'assuming intimate relations will resume as normal'.)

48 Overdoing the childproofing

Don't make the mistake of turning your house into something resembling the safe ward in a hospital for the criminally insane. Part of a baby's learning journey is exploring his environment and learning what not to touch a second time.

Preparing the Nest

Two fingers in a power point is a lesson well learned—he won't be doing that again in a hurry!

There is a plethora of stuff you can buy to childproof a house: electrical-socket covers, fences, gates, drawer stops, childproof locks, monitors, insect killers, protective mats—even a device to stop the toilet seat crashing onto a toddler's sensitive fingers. Honestly, you'd have to be pretty unlucky to have your child knocked out by a toilet seat. It's all about risk assessment, but after you've struggled with the tamper-proof lock to get into the cutlery drawer for the thirtieth time, you quickly decide that Junior can take his chances with the knives and forks.

49 Rushing out and buying a people-mover

Unless you're expecting quadruplets, don't bother. The modern world's obsession with size is extraordinary; we all think we need our houses, cars and lives to be *bigger*. Try to start your child's life off by teaching it restraint. A small car is perfectly adequate, although a towbar is not a bad idea to attach bike racks, caravans and trailers to carry equipment—nah, bugger it, get the Tarago.

50 Buying second-hand child seats

Speaking of restraint, don't stint on the child seats for the car. The baby capsules can be hired or bought for the first twelve months, but thereafter get a decent child seat and ensure it's as well maintained as the rest of the car. Actually, maybe better maintained, because when was the last time you saw a logbook? By all means try and flog it off when you've finished with it; there may be a market for seats that have been regularly soaked in urine, vomit, milk and juice, but personally I wouldn't be buying anything that smells of Glen 20 with Velcro straps covered in stubborn rusk pap.

4
HAPPY BIRTH DAY

'Well done, Mary. We all knew you had it in you.'
Dorothy Parker

(in a telegram to a friend who'd just given birth)

Use this page to draw up your birth plan. This is how you spell 'anaesthesia'.

There was a time was when childbirth was a painful trial, fraught with danger. Now it's a painful trial, fraught with choice. You can deliver your child at home, in a birthing centre, at a hospital, or by the side of the road if you don't plan adequately; in a bed, on the floor, in a bath, paddling pool or spa, on a beanbag, squatting, lying down with your legs akimbo, under a general anaesthetic or an epidural, bending over, kneeling, or upside down on a trapeze in some of the more advanced circus maternity facilities in Eastern Europe. Your birthing celebration can be attended by close friends, relatives, your Pilates instructor and of course your husband, partner or wife—gone are the days when menfolk and lesbians were banished to the waiting room to distribute the cigars. You can have your own choice of music, essential oils, Buddhist chants or whatever, and you can select to go drug-free or with any advance known to pharmaceutical science.

For the expectant parent, the day of birth becomes the sole focus. Ironic that it too soon becomes a distant memory, swamped by the ongoing demands of parenthood. It's an integral part of the species' ability to survive: the trauma recedes so we can begin to contemplate doing it again. Birth is miraculous yet ordinary, it's rarely what you expect, or are cajoled to wish for, but that doesn't matter at all. Sometimes things go wrong, but with luck, the primary goal of any birth day is the safe arrival of a healthy child—anything else is window-dressing, really. Over time, that's all you'll really remember. Can't necessarily say the same for the mother. Doubtless scarred for life, she can't wait for the child to grow old enough to understand: 'You'll never know how much pain I went through to have you!'

51 Formulating a birth plan

In my limited experience, the most pointless thing you can do is formulate a birth plan. You know the sort of thing, written on handmade paper decorated with cherubs:

> Music: *Rainforest Symphony* or Pachelbel's *Canon*
> Pain relief: Lavender compress, icepack, back massage, breathing
> Manicure during boring bits (pedicure if you can find someone willing to brave the action from that angle)
> Birth companions: Partner (obviously!), sister, best friend, second-best friend, friend who's a lesbian (for balance), mother (not in-law), father (declined for some reason), niece, that nice lady from the post office
> Birth options: Wading pool? Modular sofa?
> Readings: Shakespeare (Google appropriate quote), *Little Book of Hugs*

Stills, video and pod cast, possibly streaming on our Facebook site

Come the big day, the birth plan isn't worth the paper it's written on. By the time muggins—partner, obviously—has found somewhere to park the car within hiking distance, ransacked the car for change for the meter, unloaded all the birth-plan gear, located the birthing centre and pinpointed the correct maternity suite (a bit embarrassing to attend the wrong birth, not to mention actionable), put on the stereo, lit the oil burners and set up the cameras, mother's been whisked off for an emergency caesarean or has the nurse's arm in a pincer grip while demanding the keys to the pharmacy.

52 Reminding mother-to-be of the prenatal breathing advice

One for the expectant fathers and the first of endless mistakes that you, being male and essentially born wrong, will make on your parenting journey. I'm not sure where or when the modern trend of having the father present at the birth began, but the days of being excluded from the mystery shrouding this particular branch of secret women's business are well and truly gone. Non-attendance is not an option. Primarily, I believe, motivated by something along the lines of 'If I'm going to suffer, you're not getting off scot-free'. And yes, it is a remarkable experience to witness the birth of your children, but to be perfectly honest, moral support aside, you're about as much use in there as a skunk in a perfumery.

Our children were delivered by caesarean section (five weeks premature with their mother suffering pre-eclampsia; not good) and I was shuffled into the operating theatre in a surgical gown and a red hat that made me look like Bippo the Clown. Apparently this is done to prevent anyone thinking I was part of the theatre staff, although at that point in time it would've been hard to mistake me for anyone less qualified to be handing out the instruments or administering the gas. Back massages were not an option for me to deliver; I was simply there to hold hands and deliver words of comfort, most of those ill-chosen and poorly timed, from memory. I mean, come on, you've got to have a laugh, haven't you?

53 Videoing the procedure

Ask yourself this: outside of certain niche websites, who'd really be interested? Nothing like it to put people off the hors d'oeuvres at your first postnatal dinner party, either. Be content with your ultrasound video and some discreet stills; or at least only focus on mother from the waist up. Remember: if you're looking through the viewfinder, you're not really in the moment. And you know it'll sit there in the cupboard as twenty-three hours of raw footage that you'll never get round to editing.

54 Burning aromatherapy oils

For starters, it'd be an intense ylang-ylang oil that could cut through the industrial-grade disinfectant sprayed liberally about in hospitals in the vain hope that it might kill off the golden staph bacteria. If you're birthing at home, by all means burn all the oils you want and embrace trees as your birth celebrant reads from John Donne. However, I remain unconvinced by the power of aromatherapy to work its dubious magic in such an intense situation as the birthing room.

I find lavender oil is hard-pressed to do much to relieve the symptoms of the common cold—I doubt it'll do anything significant for you when you're pushing three and a half kilos of baby down your birth canal. Still, the nursing staff might appreciate the nice smell.

55   Going home immediately

I know many people are keen to get out of the hospital and back to their own homes, but think carefully—this is the last chance you have of a night or two with live-in childcare staff who know what they're talking about. If you think it's hard sleeping in a hospital, wait until you try it in a house with a newborn baby—assuming your anxiety and stunned disbelief let you sleep in the first place. Why not ease into motherhood with a few nights away from home? And don't fall for that modern 'We'll put baby in with mother' rubbish—demand a nursery like they had in the old movies, with puzzled fathers (usually Cary Grant) looking in the window trying to work out which one is theirs.

56   Keeping the foil balloons

No significant occasion can be marked these days without the use of helium-filled foil balloons and oversized novelty cards. Obviously, you'll want to take home memories of this special day—see the Precious Memories chapter—but remember there's nothing more depressing than a semi-deflated helium balloon drifting pathetically around the living room. This is not a time to be confronted with a metaphor for life: bouncing and joyful one minute, defeated, limp and crumpled the next.

Far better to take home something useful like the sheets or a few towels.

57 Allocating visiting rights to the extended family

Have you thought about who gets to see the baby first, especially if this is the first grandchild? What's the protocol here? When you get to the hospital, make sure the door is wide enough to allow mother and mother-in-law, cameras at the ready, to enter through it simultaneously. You're also going to be extremely tired, so don't encourage an endless stream of visitors—perhaps you could arrange a group viewing in a lounge or reception area and arrive in a dramatic fashion. Baby will of course be the centre of attention, but make sure mother gets a look-in as well; after all, you've done all the work. Fathers—forget it. Just hover in the background and look proud; no-one cares about you.

58 Assuming the children you already have will be thrilled to meet their new brother or sister

The arrival of a new sibling can be a challenging time for any child, particularly if it's the first and they're slowly realising that their brief time at the centre of the universe is about to come to an abrupt end. Before introducing them to their new brother or sister, ensure that all sharp-edged instruments have been removed from the room and that pillows, particularly of a smothering size, are closely monitored during the visit. Try to make them feel special as well—maybe buy them a gift, preferably one that can't be used as a weapon, and explain that nothing will change and you'll love them every bit as much. You're lying, of course, but try to make it sound convincing.

5

PRECIOUS MEMORIES,
OR
WHAT THE INEFFECTIVE PARENT THINKS IS WORTH KEEPING

Use this page as an afterthought to record the achievements of your middle children.

In this age of materialism, it's amazing what you'll hang onto as your child accumulates the kind of junk that weighs down every other person in the developed world. What they don't tell you in the parenting books is that you'll have to increase your household storage by the size of several shipping containers. As a child grows, naturally you can move on some of the detritus—find a smaller niece or nephew with little or no pride on whom to foist unwanted clothing as a hand-me-down wardrobe. Give generously to local charity shops, themselves just one stop on the endless loop of junk recycling that passes through school fetes, rummage sales and council clean-ups. Use the neighbours' garbage bins wisely after dark and always keep an eye out for the unattended rubbish skip. But even with the best intentions, from each stage of your child's journey through life, there will be things that you can't part with. Sentiment is a powerful force and it's all but impossible to say goodbye to so many precious mementos, even though you know deep down that a can of petrol and a match would be a merciful release. The booties, the first romper, the kindergarten artworks, the school reports chronicling years of wasted academic potential, the sporting trophies engraved 'For Having a Go!'—how could you throw all that out? So wrap them carefully, pop them away in a wardrobe and then pull them out in twenty years' time with a wondrous cry of 'Why the hell did we hang onto all this crap?'

Here are some of the things the ineffective parent will lock away in their chest of precious memories:

The Baby Years

- Identity tag from the hospital
- The deflated balloon saying 'It's a Buoy' (bought cheap in Hong Kong)
- The newspaper on that date, including Sports and My Money lift-out sections
- Baby's first solid stool
- Baby's first gift of Beatrix Potter bowl and cup (and the second, but not the third or fourth of same)
- Booties and shawl
- 75 gigabytes of photos
- 300 hours of unedited footage of baby lying down, sitting, crawling, throwing up etc.
- Commemorative birth certificate framed in native timber
- Names and phone numbers of the maternity ward staff (never referenced again)
- Lock of hair, possibly the cat's but unsure

THE TODDLER YEARS

- Child's first painting
- Child's second and third painting
- 48 indexed videotapes of baby's first steps
- Child's first painting recognisable as depicting something from nature
- Names and phone numbers of early childhood health centre staff for possible reunions (never referenced again)
- Candles from second birthday cake
- 50 gigabytes of photos
- First pair of shoes
- Novelty card from sister: 'Welcome to the Terrible Twos!'
- Tear-stained Mother's Day card from your father
- Lock of hair from first proper haircut (probably not cat's though can't be sure)

THE PRESCHOOL YEARS

- First original Mother's Day gift (hand-crafted ceramic mug made at day-care centre and bearing uncanny resemblance to first solid stool)
- First certificate for academic achievement: 'For Being Special'
- Footage of first Christmas concert, distributed via YouTube (four hits)
- Boarding pass and complimentary juice from child's first flight

- Soft toy retired from active service due to wear and unfortunate accident
- Novelty card from sister: 'Welcome to the Terrible Fours!'
- 25 gigabytes of photos
- Handmade birthday card with message in partner's poorly disguised handwriting
- Favourite picture book
- Complete boxed DVD sets of *Maisy* and *Bob the Builder* (not sure why)

THE EARLY SCHOOL YEARS

- 30-gigabyte photo spike on first day of school
- First school uniform
- First composition: 'What I Ate This Morning'
- First school photo (deluxe gift photo set with bonus wallet snaps)
- Subsequent school photos (no need for wallet snaps)
- First sporting ribbon: 'Well Done for Having a Go!'
- *Disney on Ice (Little Mermaid)* souvenir program
- School reports
- Costume worn in school play

THE LATER SCHOOL YEARS (LOSING INTEREST)

- Someone else's hat
- Sporting trophy: 'Still Having a Go'
- First mobile phone bill (let that be an example, etc.)

ROLE MODELS FOR THE INEFFECTIVE PARENT

Number One

MARY AND JOSEPH

Given what has happened in the world since his short but high-impact life, I think it's fair to say that it may have been best for Jesus to have some career guidance, perhaps a gentle hint that he should pursue carpentry with Dad rather than tackle an ill-fated crusade against the Elders of the Temple, thus inadvertently creating one of the world's largest and well, let's face it, disruptive religions. Not that I'm saying religion is in itself necessarily a bad thing (although I can happily mount a strong case for the affirmative), but I'm sure we'd have all been quite content to stick with Judaism or Buddhism or even the many gods of the Roman or Greek pantheon. Fact is, we didn't *really* need another religion at the time and perhaps a few nice tables and some decent stools would have been a much better legacy for Jesus to leave. As the lyricist Tim Rice, writing in *Jesus Christ Superstar*—frankly, all you need to know about New Testament theology—so eloquently put it:

> Nazareth your greatest son should have stayed a great unknown
> Like his father carving wood—he'd have made good
> Tables, chairs and oaken chests would have suited Jesus best
> He'd have caused nobody harm, no-one alarm.

(Bear in mind that they are words from the mouth of Judas, perhaps not the most reliable source of opinion.)

Still, having said that, what were Jesus' parents like? Well, Mary's done rather nicely out of the historical record: blessed of all women, mother of the Holy Roman Church and all that, but Joseph hasn't fared quite so well. Yes, he's a saint, bless him, but you get the feeling that Mary could've done perfectly well without him—in fact, after the story of the first Christmas in the stables, Joseph gets only one more mention in the Bible, that's Luke 2:41, recounting the time Mary and Joseph took the 12-year-old Jesus to observe the feast of the Passover in Jerusalem. To cut a long story short (and Luke does go on a bit), they were heading back to Nazareth on the ass-drawn bus or whatever it was they had back then, and a day later they noticed that Jesus wasn't with them. Must have been an extremely quiet child if it took them a whole day to notice his absence, but anyway, they hurried back to Jerusalem, only to find the young Jesus discussing theology with the priests in the Temple courts.

'I told you I'd be in my father's house,' said Jesus in all innocence, at which Joseph's face clouded over and he was heard to mutter 'Here we go again' under his breath until Mary cut him short with a stern look. Then they all went home, Joseph disappeared into the shed and that's the last we hear of him in the accredited gospels.

There are mentions of Joseph in the apocrypha, from where we also learn of the existence of Jesus' brothers—hello! Yes, apparently there were James, Joses, Simon and others, but they may have been cousins or children from a previous marriage, or perhaps Mary was visited by other angels onto a good thing—we simply don't know. In fact, we know very little about Jesus' early life because he doesn't re-enter the gospels until the age of thirty or thereabouts.

What we do know is that Mary and Joseph were not brilliant organisers. Embarrassing matter of paternity aside, they didn't look at the big picture. I know it's difficult to plan a big trip in the last stages of pregnancy, and when the Roman emperor called the census that forced them to travel to their ancestral home of Bethlehem I'm sure there was a lot of umming and aahing. But there was no booking ahead for accommodation, which meant Jesus was born in a stable—not exactly a well-managed birth plan. Thankfully, he wasn't lactose intolerant, cows being practically in the manger with him, and the presents were a bit over the top for a newborn—I didn't get myrrh until I was at least six!

Then Herod hears about this newborn King of the Jews—how did that get out? I know every parent thinks their kid is God's gift to the world, but if in the unlikely event they actually are, that sort of maternal pride is best kept for close family, and even they get sick of hearing it. Especially when it leads to some maniac demanding the death of every male child under the age of two because he feels threatened. Mind you, it certainly puts you to the top of the childcare waiting list when every other candidate has been put to the sword.

So off on the flight into Egypt—they're quite the frequent flyers in the Bible—which can't have been an easy trip with a baby, and an eventual return to Nazareth when the heat's died down. And then nothing until Jesus leaves home at the age of thirty. No-one knows how long Joseph lived, but he was certainly gone by the time Jesus began his ministry.

Did Jesus lack a decent father figure? Well, there was always God, but he was incredibly old, not what you'd call generous, and absent for most of the time. Is this another case of a strong, doting, saintly mother in the absence of a weak earthly father, or simply the predetermined fate formed by the will of an omnipotent God? Whichever it was, you wouldn't want to say no to either of them and ultimately I don't think the rest of us had any choice. We've lived with the consequences ever since.

6

DOCTORS AND NURSES

'I am sorry to say that Peter was not very well during the evening. His mother put him to bed and made him some camomile tea.'
Beatrix Potter, The Tale of Peter Rabbit

This page may be moistened and used as an emergency wipe.

No, not that sort of doctors and nurses—that's a game that comes a bit later in life and is completely natural unless they dress up a little too realistically and have extended consultations. I'm talking about the intense and ongoing relationship you'll have with your family GP as the parents of newborns. Frankly, you might as well move into the surgery because you'll be there every second day. It all begins with the early childhood health centres and the methodical recording of every medical milestone or mishap. Weight, height, peculiar rashes, ability to sit upright, regularity of bodily functions—usually no problem on that score, they're machines for it—and all the signs of normality that ineffective parents worryingly search for. Visits from the district nurse, jolly bonhomie barely disguising the faint 'I wouldn't do it like that myself' air of judgement as you struggle with baby's first bout of colic, wishing for the days when gripe water had alcohol in it and actually did something useful—i.e. put baby to sleep for three days.

From there we move into the general practitioner's world of immunisation injections, alarming fevers, ear infections (endless), grommets, dermatitis, croup, scarlet fever, impetigo, tetanus, whooping cough, chickenpox, sprains, strep throats, conjunctivitis, teething pain, moles, tonsillitis, adenoids and asthma. Then it's welcome to the casualty department and the baffling realm of triage, which is a French word meaning 'four-hour wait'. Fractures, abrasions, contusions, burns, scalds, mild poisonings, appendicitis, hernias, infected toes etc., etc.

And that's for a healthy child! God forbid the seriously ill child, that life-numbing possibility that haunts every parent, being as we are all hostages to fortune. Best not to think of that. Let's concentrate on the myriad health issues facing the 'normal' child.

While the Western world's advances in childhood health have on the whole been incredibly beneficial, they have inadvertently led to an unhealthy obsession with the state of our children's wellbeing.

59 Thinking your child is medically unusual

An easy trap to fall into, although less tempting the more children you have. Firstborns usually prove dominant and demanding in adult life for a good reason: they absorbed every moment of the anxiety of their inexperienced parents. One downside of the nuclear family is the loss of the diminishing level of paranoia that greets each new arrival. Children born fourth or later in a large family, more prevalent in yesteryear, practically bring themselves up. From a statistical point of view, there's every chance your child is completely normal, but from the very first postnatal test of vital signs you worry: are they hitting the mark? The eighth percentile band, should they be in that or would nine be better? How many kilos have they put on ... maybe three is too many! Early-onset child diabetes type two!

Look, if the child isn't walking by the age of four or has to watch the TV sideways, you might have a problem that needs medical attention. Although bear this in mind: I have a friend who didn't walk until he was three, being perfectly happy to be carried everywhere—if someone else was going to do all the work, why should he bother? Try to relax and think rationally like he did.

60 Worrying about developmental milestones

I can't tell you the number of times I've heard an ineffective parent say: 'I'm concerned about the fact that she can't crawl—she should be crawling by now' or 'He should be able to use a three-syllable word in a sentence by now'. Come off it—there are television journalists who can't do that and they've got jobs, for God's sake!

I suspect the table of developmental milestones was created by people with too much time on their hands. The more research they conducted, the more they were able to narrow the band of what is considered 'normal'. If your child waits a few months longer than the average to start talking, it means nothing more than that. If he waits until he's five years old, chances are he's a bit thick and you've wasted all that time and money on a dud.

Equally, if a child starts talking earlier than the average, it doesn't mean he's the next Shakespeare. Funnily enough, your child can reach developmental milestones quite a long way either side of the average and yet turn out to be exactly that: average. Nearly all of us do.

61 Using the internet as a medical resource

The internet is useful for many things, cheap accommodation and plentiful pornography being the two that spring most readily to mind, but for the anxious parent already hyper-alert to medical abnormality, it's a dangerous place. Using it as a medical reference can easily lead to:

62 Self-diagnosing on your child's behalf

There's a good reason doctors spend six years in medical school: it takes a while to get on top of human anatomy and physiology. You, having spent six minutes on the internet, even at high broadband speed, are unlikely be equally qualified. Misdiagnosis of a child's medical condition can be dangerous, but more usually it's merely unnecessarily worrying and time-consuming. The ineffective parent has no idea of context—we all know they often think they're the only people in the world to have reproduced—and what any GP will dismiss as wind, they'll immediately think is a twisted bowel. Surgeries and casualty departments throughout the country are filled with over-anxious parents, who are there only to be told to go home and give Junior plenty of rest and 5 millilitres of paracetamol if it hasn't cleared up by morning.

Mind you, I diagnosed red cheeks and a raised temperature as windburn. Turned out to be scarlet fever—isn't it annoying when your wife's instincts turn out to be right?

63 Excessive use of the thermometer as a diagnostic tool

Remember the old thermometers that were all but impossible to read unless held at a particular angle in reflected light during an eclipse? As a child you lived in fear of biting the glass and swallowing the mercury inside, your limbs bending into the horrendously misshapen knots of those poor Japanese children who'd eaten too much tuna laced with heavy metals. Well, I certainly did. No wonder our parents rarely used them, preferring instead to hold a hand against a burning forehead and then say, 'No, slight fever, but you'll be right for school tomorrow'. Modern thermometers, with their easy-to-read digital displays, or better still those expensive German jobs that need only a light touch to the earhole to register—they can practically do it from across the room—allow the ineffective parent to monitor their child's temperature to within a percentage point of one degree Celsius. Fact of the matter is, a child's metabolism goes up and down like a yoyo. Unless it's unusually high over a period of time, simply hydrate and apply a wet flannel. Monitor the situation, then eventually do the emergency dash to the doctor with your partner saying 'I told you so, you never listen to me' and so on and so forth.

64 Inventing medical problems for your child

There is only one thing worse than hypochondria and that is hypochondria by proxy. The rare medical condition known as Munchausen syndrome is named after the eighteenth-century Baron Karl Friedrich Hieronymus Freiherr von Münchhausen. (Imagine trying to fit that on the back of your cardigan or your lunchbox name label.) The baron was an inveterate storyteller, a fantasist who invented glamorous and exciting fictions about himself and his personal exploits. Munchausen syndrome was first recognised in patients repeatedly fronting up for medical procedures, inventing symptoms or even harming themselves in order to gain the sympathy and attention of the medical fraternity.

Take that obsession one step further and you have Munchausen syndrome by proxy, in which the sufferers invent symptoms in someone else, usually their children. This can be very dangerous and is difficult to delineate from abuse; when does mild poisoning to necessitate a trip to the hospital for the attention and excitement become an actual attempt to harm? Almost immediately, I'd guess.

Personally, I'm the reverse. I deny symptoms in my children simply so they'll go to school and get out of the house.

65 Creating allergies for your child

A study by the American advocacy group Food Allergy & Anaphylaxis Network and reported in the *Boston Globe* found that, while 25 per cent of surveyed parents thought their children had food allergies, in fact only 4 per cent did. Severe reactions to certain foods, most commonly peanuts, tree nuts and shellfish, are a serious problem for those children unlucky enough to suffer them. Artificially inflating the problem in the wider community through general hysteria and ignorance does nothing to help those sufferers.

For a start, true allergies are often confused with food intolerance, which in turn is confused with food aversion or dislike. (It's generally accepted that children will dislike 90 per cent of foodstuffs even before they've tasted, sighted, smelled or in some cases heard of them.) True allergies provoke a response from the immune system that produces antibodies and histamines, which in the most extreme cases lead to anaphylactic shock, possibly causing death, although the rate of food-allergy death in the United States is comparable to death by lightning strike. Neither is ideal.

Young children who prove to be allergic to milk, soya or eggs generally outgrow those allergies within five to ten years; shellfish and peanut and other nut allergies tend to last a lot longer, although it's now estimated that perhaps 20 per cent of child sufferers will outgrow the condition. Diagnosis is difficult because skin-prick tests are inconclusive, often only indicating a likelihood that has to be further tested by ingested exposure to the offending foodstuff under controlled conditions. Understandably, some parents are reluctant to go that far. However, incorrect diagnosis can have a powerful effect; a 2003 US study found that children who were told they were peanut allergic felt greater anxiety and physical restriction than children with juvenile diabetes.

Funnily enough, alternative medical practitioners are more likely to ascribe symptoms to food allergies than genuine—sorry, mainstream—doctors. Although it makes sense; if you have no idea what is causing a rash, why not blame a walnut? This may also account for the perceived 'outbreak' of peanut intolerance, although many studies conclude there is no significant rise in true food allergies, with levels across the population continuing to hover at 4 per cent. So be wary of over-anxious parents who want to ban non-organic chicken strips from the canteen menu because Tarquin is allergic to imported breadcrumbs, particularly if he's just been to see an aromatherapist.

And here are some interesting statistics from a French survey of food-allergy sufferers: 63 per cent were female and 80 per cent were urban dwellers. Which leads us to the next point:

66 Obsessively worrying about 'hygiene'

Children who grow up on farms, regularly exposed to dirt, animals, dung, mud and possibly foreclosure develop a stronger autoimmune system than those children shielded from life's unpleasantness by antibacterial wipes, antiseptic soaps and a decent sewerage system. Exposure to bacteria in the early years is a vital part of strengthening your child's ability to fight disease, so you do him or her no favours by bathing the plastic dinosaurs in Dettol and adding Pine O Cleen to the playdough recipe. On the other hand, don't go overboard and drag them backwards through their own excrement. They're perfectly capable of doing that themselves.

67 Comparing your child's health and development with others

Like comparing children in general, this is not a good idea. Obviously, if the other kids are running about and your child can't move to a standing position, a comparison may be useful, but as a rule, try to avoid it. It just makes your child feel inadequate—which they may well be, but there's no need to rub it in.

68 Thinking an itchy head is due to flaky scalp

Sorry, it's nits. And you'd better get used to the idea because they're going to be with you for years. It doesn't matter how clean your child's hair is—ironically, head lice prefer cleaner hair—or how vigilant you are in avoiding contact with nit-infested classmates, you can't avoid them. And they are strangely persistent creatures, growing resistant to nearly all chemical treatments. Personally, we found the most effective treatment was an electronic comb, relishing the destructive force of 1.5 volts of raw power surging through their tiny insect bodies as they convulsed, helpless in its grip, their feeble nit voices crying out in one last wail of despair. The other advantage is you can have a useful maths session with your child (no opportunity should be passed up for learning fun!) as you count the charred remains. Just bear in mind that not many kindergarten kids can add up to fifty.

69 Trusting in the alternative nit treatment you bought at the organic market

Don't even bother. Lavender and patchouli oil aren't going to touch them. I'm always bewildered that those promoting the soft benevolence of 'natural' products seem to forget that arsenic, acid and hemlock are 'natural' as well. Mind you, *they* probably would get rid of the head lice.

Children have not escaped society's faddish swing to New Age remedies. Personally, I'm sceptical, reluctant to disregard the benefits of Western medicine. I can't see much point in returning to the good old days of 60 per cent child mortality or crippling polio, despite the ability to jump puddles and wear a defiant grin. For a short time in our neighbourhood we boasted a New Age children's shop that sold, among other things, organic cots. How a cot can be certified organic is beyond me—maybe the steel components were forged without insecticides—but there it was, alongside the organic nappies, recyclable prams that resembled space docking modules and sensible play clothes made out of hemp by the indigenous people of Peru. Needless to say, the prices were far from organic and the business model proved unsustainable.

However, some parents insist on treating their children as New Age laboratories, happily testing alternative remedies on them that have not been systematically tested on anything else. At their most extreme, these 'treatments', usually in the form of fad diets or the refusal of medical intervention, can lead to hospitalisation or even death. This is not to suggest that massaging baby with ionised almond oil and bergamot is going to cause asthma, but it sure as hell isn't going to cure it either.

70 Not having your child immunised

Immunisation is one of the great success stories of modern medicine. In developed countries, it has greatly reduced the rates of diphtheria, polio, rubella, tetanus, hepatitis, mumps, pertussis (whooping cough) and chickenpox. (Progress is understandably slower in the developing world.) Vaccines have been developed against meningococcal disease, meningitis and rotavirus, a common cause of diarrhoea. Diseases such as smallpox have all but been eliminated from the planet. Immunisation is an overwhelmingly beneficial procedure, yet persistent ill-founded fears about its safety threaten its efficacy; it only works when as many people as possible are vaccinated, yet some parents refuse on their child's behalf.

They do so for a number of reasons, ranging from religious beliefs to fears about unanticipated side effects. For example, some religious groups object to key ingredients of the vaccines, most particularly the gelatine that is added as a stabiliser against extreme temperature variations. The gelatine is usually of bovine or porcine origin and the fact that it might have come from pigs is enough to put some Jewish and Islamic parents right off. Rest easy, fundamentalists, for scholars of the Islamic Organization for Medical Sciences have decided that the pork products are so transmuted in the process of being turned into gelatine as to render them safe to be injected into observant Muslims. Likewise, the Jewish religious authorities have given vaccines containing gelatine the green light. The clearance of the bacon and egg roll, however, remains a long way off.

(Speaking of eggs, those with egg allergies shouldn't be given vaccines for influenza or yellow fever, or a particular type of rabies vaccine, grown, as they are, in eggs. If in any doubt, consult your GP, who will refer you to specialist immunisation centres.)

Similarly, some devout Catholics have ethical and moral objections to the process of laboratory cell line culturing of some vaccines in Australia because the cells used were taken from three elective abortions performed for medical reasons in the 1960s. Tempting as it is to just say, 'Alright, forget it, hand your child over to the care of a loving and benevolent God', the Vatican has seen reason—and that's not a phrase you read very often—and allowed the use of such vaccines on a temporary basis, especially with regard to rubella.

Religious types aside, keen as they are to instil dogma into children who can't even point to their belly buttons, let alone decide for themselves if the universe is a deist, theist or arbitrary creation, there are others who fear immunisation.

They believe it can cause cancer, asthma, reduced immunity, diabetes—even HIV-AIDS. This last superstition was based on an erroneous report that a polio vaccine used in the 1950s contained SIV, a virus found in monkeys, which in turn gave the vaccine recipients HIV-1 and caused the first outbreak of AIDS. Exhaustive testing found no traces of SIV in the vaccines.

But it doesn't stop there. Vaccines are blamed for SIDS, multiple sclerosis and autism, parents' fears targeting, as they often do, diseases and conditions of unknown or uncertain causes. What better to blame than the mysterious 'bacteria' injected into their baby's arm? If the child has a convulsion an hour later, what further proof is required? Reason often flies out the window where one's children are concerned; one forgets that the child could just as easily have had the convulsion without the injection and coincidence of timing is no proof of causality at all.

Some diehards maintain that immunisation has nothing to do with reduced disease rates, that it's all due to improved sanitation and healthier lifestyles. I'm reminded of the story of the American jogger who was bitten by a rabid fox and then ran for another two kilometres with the fox, refusing to let go, firmly attached to her arm. She then drove herself and the fox to hospital. First thing she sensibly asked for, despite her obvious triathlon super-fitness and healthy lifestyle, was a rabies and tetanus shot. The fox, I believe, discharged itself and went to a naturopath.

Occasionally, studies *will* highlight problems with certain ingredients of vaccines—a mercury-based preservative called thiomersal was withdrawn in 2000 because of concerns over the mercury levels it could lead to in underweight babies receiving the shots. Even so, there's probably more mercury in a tuna sandwich. An older style of oral polio vaccine very rarely caused vaccine-associated paralytic polio (VAPP), but the overall risk of infection was calculated at one in 2.4 *million*. It was replaced by an alternative polio vaccine in Australia in 2005 to avoid this rare side effect.

But none of the perceived risks or the brief moment of pain can ever outweigh the benefits. Or, indeed, the reduced risk of your child contracting a painful and potentially dangerous condition in later life. Measles, for example, is a nasty disease that most of us have forgotten about, largely due to the success of the immunisation program. One in seventy measles sufferers requires hospitalisation—it can even kill. There was a spike in the incidence of measles in Australia during the tour of a spiritual group who were not immunised (funny, that); likewise, most of the people who attended their meetings were not immunised either. They've yet to work out just what God was telling them.

But why, you ask, do some children who have been immunised get chickenpox? Well, the vaccine is not 100 per cent effective. And ironically, the more people who refuse to be immunised, the greater the chance of everybody else being exposed to the disease. The reverse is known as 'herd immunity'—the more people are immunised, the more protection there is for those vulnerable people who cannot be vaccinated for medical reasons. Don't for one minute think that because the common diseases of our childhood— mumps, measles, chickenpox and even polio—have all but disappeared that they've gone for good. No, they're lurking about somewhere, waiting for us to slacken off on the immunisation effort.

Now before I sound like a paid advertisement for the health department, let me conclude by heartily recommending you get your child immunised. Ignore the myth makers and religious nuts, the conspiracy theorists and the ill-informed; do it for your child's wellbeing and the good health of society as a whole.

7

BEDTIME

'People who say they sleep like a baby usually don't have one.'
Les J Burke

This page can be randomly vandalised by your child.

Sleep, precious sleep. Like chocolate or crack-cocaine, you don't know how much you want it until you can't get it. Sleep deprivation would have to be the number one complaint of any new parent, but you'll just have to put up with it, unless you're one of the lucky ones that gets a child who sleeps through without much fuss. Pity the others lumbered with the child that doesn't want—or apparently need—any sleep lasting more than twenty minutes. Thankfully, most kids fall somewhere in the middle. Establishing a reliable sleep and bedtime routine will pay big dividends in the future, so get on top of it as soon as you can.

71 Boasting of how your child slept through from the age of two months

That's a bare-faced lie and even if it's true no-one wants to hear it, especially when they're only seconds away from violent irrational behaviour because their eyelids are held open with matchsticks. And don't forget that as a general rule, you always find a sympathetic ear when you tell anyone how awful your kids are, but you'll never get the same reception when you go on about how wonderful they can be.

And you lucky ones with the babies who sleep through, beware—the sleep patterns of children change quickly. At about nine months, even the soundest of sleepers may begin waking and crying during the night. Apparently, this is the time when babies begin to realise that you still exist even when they can't see you—God knows what they've been thinking up to that point. They now know you're in the next room and demand your presence. From now on there's nowhere to hide.

72 Allowing your baby to sleep whenever and wherever it wants

In the first few months of life, babies tend to sleep after feeding and are usually happy to do it wherever the mood takes them. But eventually the child's periods of wakefulness take on a pattern and it's best if you can shape this pattern into something resembling the daily running of your household: i.e. we sleep at night and do stuff during the day. Some babies confuse day and night but can be quickly reprogrammed—feed and play during the day; less fanfare and fun as the sky darkens. By about four months, babies should start to get used to falling asleep in their own beds without company, so encourage them to do so. Begin as you mean to go on.

73 Making the baby's cot look 'nice'

Don't over-decorate the child's cot. By now, all parents should be aware of the basic rules to help prevent SIDS. In case you need reminding, here are they are:

- Always put the child to sleep on his back
- Remove all soft and fluffy blankets, quilts, toys, pillows and bolsters
- Make up the cot so the child is sleeping towards the bottom end
- Use safety-approved cots or bassinettes
- Don't over-dress the baby—overheating increases the risk
- Don't expose your child to second-hand cigarette smoke

And that rules out first-hand smoke as well, so if baby's got a pack-a-day habit, get her to cut down.

74 Thinking that the baby has to sleep in the same room as you do

As long as you are within earshot of the baby, there is no reason for the child to sleep in the same room. It's understandable for the nervous parent to want to be able to hear every snort, grunt or irregular breathing pattern—for months I would go in on a regular basis and check that they were still breathing. An intercom system may be of help here. I know of one couple who took the intercom receiver over to the pub with them—the range on some of these things is remarkable. Train your baby to push the button and say, 'All fine in here. Over and out'.

Of course, there's no rule that says you can't have the child in the room with you, but remember: years down the track, you don't want to hear: 'Can you two keep it down? I'm trying to watch *Lateline*'.

75 Having the child sleep in the bed with you

There's nothing like the warmth and delight of a sleeping infant beside you and evidence suggests that it does no long-term damage to the child—in many cultures they all bunk down together, although the practice may have been born of necessity rather than anything else, there not being many spare rooms in a tent. And it's certainly a crude but effective form of contraception. Personally, I wouldn't make it a long-term habit; the warmth and delight factor has well and truly cooled when they hit their teens. Ideally, you want your child to sleep securely and confidently in its own bed and unless you begin early, it's a very difficult habit to form in later life.

76 Not establishing a bedtime routine

Some parents shy away from setting a regular bedtime for their children—those who are night owls want to spend quality time with their kids when they themselves feel most relaxed. That's marvellous, except for the fact that the parents don't need between eight and thirteen hours' sleep a night and they don't have to get up and go to school in the morning. Do your kid a favour and get them into the routine of cleaning their teeth and going to bed at a reasonable hour when they're asked to.

77 Stressing about the daytime nap schedule

Any respite from a new child is welcome and their morning and afternoon naps quickly become oases of calm for the household, with mother snoring gently beside the sleeping child. Children grow out of the need for naps at different times—some as soon as nine months, others hanging on to sweet Morpheus's daytime embrace for years—and they resent being forced into a sleeping schedule they no longer benefit from. Two naps a day soon becomes one and then none at all. Use your common sense and when baby no longer wants a morning nap say in a gentle yet firm voice: 'You do what you want, but excuse me while I lie down and stack up a few Z's'.

78 Immediately comforting the crying child

A baby who is instantly comforted when she cries quickly gets used to the idea. Why sit on the floor when a brief wail will have you up on mother's hip? There are plenty of genuine reasons for crying—all kids do it—but these usually begin to diminish at a few months of age as early discomforts like colic and indigestion are left behind and the child becomes more aware of its surroundings and begins to self-regulate its moods. Even so, bedtime can be a difficult time for a young child, particularly if it enjoys the undivided attention of at least one parent when it's awake. The first response to being left alone in a room can be, unsurprisingly, to cry. Reassure the wailing infant, then leave. The child has to learn how to put himself to sleep—if he gets rocking, patting and soothing for hours, that's what he'll get used to and he'll demand it every night.

There is a technique for dealing with this at an early stage (it's generally agreed, though, that it shouldn't be attempted with babies under six months). It was once called 'controlled crying', but with appropriate political correctness it's now referred to as 'controlled comforting'. Essentially, it's a system whereby you allow the child to cry without being placated for increasingly long periods of time (over however many nights it takes) until they realise you're not going to come in and they think 'Sod you, then' and go to sleep anyway. In my experience, it's a wrenching and traumatic thing to do—but only for the parents. The child, beyond some minor disgruntlement, doesn't appear to suffer at all and you'll be amazed at how successful the procedure can be.

However, it must be said that there are those who disagree and disapprove of any child being allowed to cry at all. The words 'zealots' and 'misguided' spring to mind.

79 Worrying about dummies

Another point of endless debate—are dummies, or pacifiers, harmful? Having trodden on a few as I stumbled in the dark to retrieve them for a wailing infant, I can say yes. But in the greater scheme of things, I can't really see any harm in a baby sucking on a dummy—it's better than a baby bottle full of Coke. Some children take to dummies; others spit them out. But bear in mind that, if you do go down the dummy route, it's very hard for the child when they reach the point of saying goodbye to their oral comforters. Respect the child's concerns and make the separation a special moment—I believe we posted the final pacifier to a horse. He never wrote back to say if he'd received it.

80 Dismissing your child's night-time fears

I've tried it and I can tell you it doesn't work. For some reason the children cannot see the inherent illogic in worrying that tigers are going to escape from the zoo, find out where we live, scale the wall to the second storey then ease through a small window and eat them. What's not to understand? How could a tiger possibly ask for directions to our house? I mean, what are the chances of him finding someone who knows us, for a start? And yes, while I encourage your childlike innocent belief in Santa Claus and the tooth fairy, there are no such things as monsters or witches who can actually do anything vaguely frightening outside of books.

No, for some reason they just don't get it. Listen to their fears, gently explain that the house is surrounded by a magic force-field called love that no evil can penetrate, then put on a Harry Potter tape to calm them off to sleep.

81 Giving your child red drinks after 3 p.m.

I don't know what they put in it—and I don't think I want to—but there is something about a red drink that transports a child to a parallel universe where perpetual motion is de rigueur. I always thought it a fanciful old wives' tale, but now that I know more old wives, I see their point. As a general rule, don't overstimulate your child before bedtime. Discourage bouncing, cartwheels and video games like *Bouncing Hyper-Cartwheel Mario Brothers* after dinner.

82 Indulging the child who suddenly won't sleep in their own bed

This is a behavioural change that can kick in at about eight or nine years of age. It often presents as night-time fears or the onset of supposed physical symptoms like a sore throat or stomach-ache. Like the boy who cried wolf, it's a tricky one to spot, but knock it on the head right then and there.

You can use a variation on the controlled-comforting technique—offer to stay in their room with them for twenty minutes each night for a week; at the doorway for twenty minutes the next week; down the hall the next and so on, a little further each time until you're in Paris.

8
THE CREATIVE CHILD

'If children grew up according to early indications,
we should have nothing but geniuses.'
Goethe

This page is a blank canvas for your child's latent genius.

Spot on, Goethe—and nothing's changed in 200 years. Given the number of supposedly gifted and talented youngsters in our schools today, we are surely in for an extraordinary renaissance when their latent artistic genius finally buds. Has there ever been such a legion of creative children? No primary school is worth its salt if it can't offer band programs, choirs, drama classes, art courses, experts-in-residence, dance and creative writing so all the junior Beethovens, Bussells and De Niros can explore their full potential.

83 Thinking your child is gifted and talented

It may well be, but the odds overwhelmingly suggest that it isn't. There is a current mania for gifted and talented children; every second parent assumes they have at least one, forgetting that if everyone was gifted and talented, relatively no-one would be. It's perfectly understandable to want to see the best in your child, but try to be reasonable—are they just bright and engaged? If they can read and enjoy Proust by Year 4, you might have something on your hands, but beware of jumping to conclusions. For example, most children can play a recorder if pressed—many people can even survive having to listen to it—but a precocious ability to play 'London's Burning' at the age of four does not make you the next Mozart. When you've written a piano concerto at five, come back and talk to me.

84 Forcing your child to behave as if they were gifted and talented

Speaking of Mozart, did his father make him practise six hours a day and show off his unusual prowess? Well, actually, yes, he did, but that's not the point—he was the exception that proves the rule. In my experience, the more the parent protests the child's genius, the less well founded the claim turns out to be. Too often, the disappointments of a parent's own thwarted creative career are channelled into the child: 'I never got the chance to follow my dream of [insert fantasy here], but I'm going to make sure you do'. For a brief moment, the confused child thinks 'Brilliant! We're getting cable TV!' but then is sadly brought back to earth with four hours' practice of 'London's Burning'.

85 Worrying that your child will be unfulfilled if they're not artistic in some way

Trust me, they'll probably be more unfulfilled in later life if they are. There is nothing worse than the non-realisation of a perceived artistic talent. Ask any waiter. The role of the artist in society is a vital one—no, come on, it is—but it is a difficult and lonely calling. I suspect it's sought after by parents because it marks their child out as being *different*.

Okay, if that's your thing, why not encourage them to identify as a Venezuelan?

Relentlessly pushing your child to an artistic goal may deprive them of the joy of arriving there themselves, or not allow them to pursue the arts as a delightful hobby rather than an onerous calling. Far better to point your child in the direction of something useful like science, or something pointless but fabulously well paid like commercial law.

86 Encouraging craft sessions

There is a general conspiracy by the members of the craft accessories manufacturing industry to encourage parents to engage their children in craft on a daily, if not hourly, basis. I don't know from where this notion that an ability to do craft badly in some way improves you as a human being came, but I do wish it would go back. It all looks so easy on *Play School*—until you finally twig that the reason it appears effortless and fun is that there are no children involved. Of course, you could get up at night with your husband and make a set of dolls-house furniture out of toilet rolls and iceblock sticks while the kids are safely asleep, but no doubt you have better things to do. And when you attempt craft with the kids present, it quickly descends into a paste-sodden free-for-all that ends with them inhaling glitter and your misshapen cardboard efforts bearing no resemblance at all to the planets in the solar system or whatever they were meant to represent. By all means attempt craft in a plastic-lined room with adequate drainage; otherwise leave well alone until the children are old enough to get work as *Play School* presenters, where it may be of some practical use.

87 Telling your child that four legs and a mane don't necessarily make it look like a horse

Apparently, you're not allowed to tell kids the truth about their artwork. You really have to bite your tongue and encourage their feeble scrawling. Remember how tentative your first attempts at figurative representation were; recall how pathetic they are even now. I quite enjoyed drawing with our two when they were small, in hindsight probably more than they did because they inevitably drifted away to do something else while I was still colouring Bob the Builder without going outside the lines. Even if I say so myself, I became quite a dab hand with a sketch—my polar bear with cub has become almost recognisable to anyone without too much additional prompting.

But there is a school of thought that suggests you don't circumscribe your child's drawing or painting by insisting that it look like something. Ironically, they reach that conclusion independently and frustration sets in as they struggle for representational detail. Encourage them to keep at it; anything difficult takes time. And don't reward anything put together on the computer—where's the challenge in click-and-drag colouring in? Get them started on the hard stuff like pencil and paper or etching with acid. Maybe not. And remember: anyone who can make a half-decent dinosaur out of plasticine deserves a medal.

88 Plastering the walls and fridge door with your children's artwork

Yes, I know they need encouragement, but don't overdo it. Their initial pride at seeing their work displayed can quickly descend to a world-weary insouciance; 'I've exhibited now on the fridge, basically I've achieved what I wanted to do with my art. Everything else is just a sell-out'.

89 Regarding paint by numbers as patronising

Nothing could be further from the truth. Kids love boundaries and a helping hand, so these kits can be useful. And if they slap enough paint on, you can't see the numbers underneath and everyone thinks they did it themselves. Look—Monet's haystacks and she's only five!

90 Introducing the concept of novelty stationery

Most children love to collect pencils, textas and rubbers—in fact a texta only has to be used once to be declared no good any more and a replacement demanded. Our house now contains enough partly used coloured pencils to build a small raft. Canny merchandisers have latched onto this, as indeed they have with so many aspects of child psychology, taking advantage of the Chinese economic miracle to manufacture endless amounts of cheap rubbish to fill party bags, supermarket checkouts and two-dollar shops. They're particularly fond of the collectible lines, drip-feeding a seemingly inexhaustible supply of products into the shops that children *have* to buy. My children were sucked into the Smiggle line of stationery products, novelty erasers, pencils and paper that were scented like bubblegum. This stuff even has its own chain of stores! Teams of small girls plan shopping expeditions simply to buy Smiggle.

Of course it's justified because it's a 'creative' toy. Yes indeed, pencil and paper can be creative tools: if you use them. Simply amassing vast stockpiles of the stuff somewhat defeats the purpose.

91 Enrolling your child in Leesa-Mayree's School of Dance

First up, be immediately wary of anyone with an oddly spelt name. Secondly, anyone who teaches hip-hop to people under the age of ten should be taken out and shot. There's enough of that sort of thing in real life without seeing it up on the stage. Have you ever endured a dance school end-of-year concert? An endless procession of rhythmically challenged girls doing cartwheels every other step, with one, possibly two, self-conscious boys in unitards hovering up the back. People are known to gnaw their own arms off in order to escape when, three hours in, they realise it's only up to the under-sevens. Having said that, it's amazing that people who are outraged by the work of photographer Bill Henson are more than happy to watch their 6-year-old daughters dressed like hookers doing a jazz-ballet routine to 'Don't Cha Wish Your Girlfriend Was Hot Like Me?', while complete strangers record the whole thing on video.

92 Enrolling your child in classical ballet

Every little girl dreams of being a ballerina, even the heftier ones who are fooling themselves. And the success of *Billy Elliot* has lifted the number of boys doing classical dance to, well, at least eight. The ballet is without doubt a beautiful and elegant art form, but in the long run it will do your child more physical harm than playing rugby league, although the incidence of sexual assault is lower and it's certainly more artistic. Ballet is unnatural; no-one was made to bend and straighten in that particular fashion, and hip joints have long memories. By all means buy your child a tutu, comb their hair back so tightly it's practically leaving their scalp and encourage them to skip about to 'The Dance of the Sugar Plum Fairies', but think long and hard about sending them off to ballet school. On the plus side, if they get into the national school, they leave home at twelve.

93 Buying expensive musical instruments without a trial period

Saxophones, drum kits, euphoniums, glockenspiels, grand pianos—all bought with such high hopes and expectations, only to be abandoned after three weeks and twenty minutes of desultory practice. And here's a tip: Cash Converters aren't that interested in glockenspiels. The gift of musicianship is a wonderful thing, but don't confuse being able to appreciate music with being able to play it. Compare the number of capable musicians with the number of video-game players—it's tiny! Reason being that musical ability is rare, while the ability to sit on your fat arse in front of a TV shooting things is unsurprisingly common.

Make sure your child really wants to play music before investing in the instrument. (If she's keen to play triangle, you could probably risk that.) Rent or borrow the more expensive instrument for a few months, then return it and try something else. Work your way through the orchestral groups: brass, strings, woodwind and, if you absolutely have to, percussion. Then abandon all hope and get the child a new Xbox. Or a GarageBand program for your computer;

then they can pretend it's them writing and playing the music instead of the machine.

However, if you insist on pushing through with this, here are same basic traps to avoid:

94 Saying: 'It's okay, you don't have to learn to read music'

There are some successful musicians who can't read or write musical notation—none in any of the quality orchestras as far as I know—but they are few and far between and are usually blessed with either a fantastic ear or innate musicianship. For the rest of us, if we can't read music we eventually reach a brick wall and our musical progress comes to a halt. If your kid is serious about music, encourage her to learn to read it, slow and difficult as the journey may be. Believe me, like learning anything else, it gets a lot harder once you get older.

95 Saying: 'Tell you what, I'll learn the piano at the same time!'

Just too painful for all concerned. You'll want to practise even less than they do. Plus there's the humiliation of being the only person at the third grade exam over the age of nine.

96 Saying: 'Of course you can learn the drums!'

Pots and pans in the kitchen—that delicious moment when you realise that baby is actually coordinating those erratic arm movements with some kind of plan. Clapping in time with Big Ted (although it's a bit hard to hear those soft paws beating a rhythm) or stomping along to the mind-numbing drum machine of Hi-5—my God, the child is the next Keith Moon! But in a good, not drug-addicted, substance-abusing, dead-by-the-age-of-forty way! Quickly, line the spare rooms with egg cartons and get down to Billy Hyde Drum Clinic with all speed. Max out the credit card, set up the kit, endure weeks of ear-splitting noise, lose the love of the neighbours, then put the lot up for sale in the *Trading Post* when Junior loses interest. Or worse, if he succeeds in mastering the skins, condemn him to a lifetime of being the butt of every muso joke (along with banjo and viola players) and the last out of every pub gig because he's still packing up.

97   Telling your child the clarinet is cool

It's an outrageous lie and no-one's made a go of clarinet playing since Acker Bilk. Yes, Woody Allen plays the clarinet, but his later clarinet playing is nowhere near as good as his early stuff. And would you really want him teaching your teenager how to purse and blow?

98   Encouraging your child to dream of auditioning for *Australian Idol*

There are two schools of thought about the *Idol* reality-TV franchise—one that believes the program is nothing more than a cheap, derivative and lazy marketing scheme to sell records, and the other that believes it is. If there is anything to be gained from artistic talent it is creativity—slavishly emulating the style and work of others is little more than glorified karaoke. Of course, each successive generation faces the dilemma of the back catalogue—it's all been done before and emulation becomes harder to avoid. But do try to encourage your child to use art to discover something unique about themselves and not surrender as cannon fodder to the 'entertainment industry'. Of course they'll die poor and/or insane, but at least they'll peg out with honour.

9

DAY-CARE DREAMING

'I love children, especially when they cry, for then someone takes them away.'
Nancy Mitford

This page can be used as a travel bib.

With today's busy lifestyles and the economic pressures of the two-income household, many parents have to place their children into childcare at an early age. (And I'm no economist, but what came first—economic pressures or two incomes?) In fact, some kids are so swiftly sent to long day care, you wonder why the parents bothered having them in the first place. But there will come a time for many—if not most—parents when a child has to be placed into care for at least one or two days a week.

Opinion is mixed on the effects of childcare on small children. Leaving your child in the care of others can be an emotive issue and studies into the effects of extended childcare can appear contradictory. For its part, the government encourages childcare to ensure maximum involvement in the workforce, but levels of paid maternity (or paternity) leave vary widely in the world and many parents experience difficulty in finding places and then paying the fees.

What to choose? The community-based centre, where your child will be exposed to vegetarianism, social-democratic politics, homeopathic treatments and playmates with two mothers or, far less commonly, two fathers? The corporate childcare facility, where the only people you get to meet are receivership administrators and liquidators? Or a home-based child-minding service run by a large retiree of European descent who smells vaguely of garlic? After months of being on every available waiting list, you'll take anything.

But do watch out for these pitfalls:

99 Selecting a childcare centre on a least-cost basis

I know a person who knows a person who selects wine in a restaurant without bothering to consult the wine list; she simply asks for: 'White, second cheapest'. And I dare say that's a perfectly satisfactory way of ordering wine. It might not work quite so well when choosing where to entrust the safety of your child, but if you go with accredited, licensed facilities that appear to have at least one fire exit and adequate guttering, second cheapest will probably be as good as any other.

Childcare is such an expensive proposition that, even should they manage to negotiate any form of government rebate, parents are often forced into a low-cost option. It doesn't necessarily mean poor-quality care: childcare is more about the staff than the premises. Look for a centre that doesn't have a high rotation of staff; where the people are ones you'd be prepared to spend eight hours a day with. Are they qualified, with appropriate police checks? Do they provide a decent lunch and water-based paints? Do they have any places available, like, now?

100 Believing a brightly coloured centre is a jolly place for baby

The corporatisation of childcare in Australia has not been an entirely successful experiment—personally, the concept of shareholders making money out of other people caring for other people's children never seemed a good idea to me. And, as it turned out, it wasn't. However, the legacy of a corporate approach to childcare-centre design lingers: brightly coloured feature walls, Disney-character murals and perky, underpaid staff. If I was a small child, I'd find that much pink and bright blue nauseating—it'd put me right off my bananas and custard and I'd always thereafter subliminally connect the Little Mermaid with a faltering start at toilet training.

101 Putting a 2-month-old child into extended day care

Touchy area, this one, and everyone has a different opinion, but I'm going to go out on a limb. Is this such a good idea? Could there not have been a little more planning beforehand? I know returning to work is often an imperative, particularly for single parents, but is there a member of the extended family who can help out? If there are a few children involved, would it be actually cheaper to hire in-home help? And yes, I know the thought of a hard day's work can seem like a holiday compared to the demands of small children—sometimes the thought of sitting in a cesspit with pins in your eyes seems a more attractive option. But ideally, one or the other of a child's parents should be with him in the early months.

However, having said all that, I know of no definitive studies that find children are lastingly damaged by being placed into care at an early age, so if you have to do it, don't compound your problems by worrying about it.

102 Trying to work out the government's childcare rebate scheme

Like many bureaucratic processes, the form required to enter the childcare rebate scheme is designed to put you off applying. For starters, it's longer than the Old Testament and requires a far more extensive genealogy. Be prepared to provide greater proof of your existence than you ever knew was possible. Blood samples and the promise of the soul of your firstborn may help speed your application. Living as I do in the freelance world, it's all but impossible to calculate income—it's almost as hard as it is to make it—but make sure you don't underestimate your earnings. Any mistakes are rewarded with years of correspondence, veiled threats and new, yet even more complicated, forms.

103 Assuming that your business meeting will end at 5.45 p.m.

You know deep down it'll go longer and you'll be in a blind panic to get to the childcare centre on time because they charge like wounded bulls for every minute after closing time. Try to schedule your work day to give you plenty of time for drop-off, settling time and pick-up. Avoid allowing your child to be the first one there and the last to leave; the staff may think you're uninterested. At my children's day-care centre, one of the fathers would arrive at 5.30 and then sit in his car making phone calls and reading the newspaper until the strike of closing time at 6 p.m. Obviously keen to spend quality time with his precious children.

104 Thinking that your involvement with a day-care centre ends with signing the cheque

Many day-care centres, especially not-for-profit or community centres, rely on the active support of the parents—ditto schools in later life. Volunteer for working bees or help out at the Christmas party. Your children will welcome the involvement and you can all gossip self-righteously about the parents who didn't bother to turn up as you rake leaves, scrub tables and decontaminate the sandpit.

105 Hiring a foreign exchange student as a live-in nanny

Fraught with difficulty, even though attractive as a potentially low-cost option. I know many parents have had a delightful experience with Inge or Anna-Freda living in for six months as they learn English, but think twice about this course of action. Have you got enough room for another person in the household? Studies show that most 18-year-old Swedes do not consider bunk beds in the kids' room as independent accommodation. Nor do they consider bedding down with the bosses as part of the deal, although if you can find someone willing to give it a shot, why not?

Carefully read the fine print of the arrangement. These schemes usually stipulate a number of hours that are expected in return for board and a modest salary; don't expect them to be on tap as babysitters. Their hours will be quickly absorbed in the daily running of the family and it'll be them having a good night out five times a week.

106 Using the cinema as a child-minding service

The mums-and-bubs matinees are a common feature at many cinemas and, because other patrons have been duly warned that they won't be able to concentrate on the film at all, by all means take your baby or toddler along. I did, but found the experience to be a bit like a sofa bed, which is neither a comfortable sofa nor an adequate bed. Basically it became a competition to see who could be louder: the soundtrack or the wailing children.

But don't think you can take your child anywhere. Would you like your evening cinema experience to be compromised by a crying child? Would you be thrilled to be travelling first class, only to find a 9-month-old infant projectile vomiting over your sky-bed and suffering earache for twelve hours?

107 Leaving baby with the neighbours

Awkward, especially if you haven't asked them before you do it. Sometimes an elderly neighbour will offer to help, glad to have the company of even a two-year-old. Your child, however, may tire of hearing stories of how the world was before mobile phones, television and the welfare state. Ensure that your neighbour is sound in body and mind and can remember emergency numbers. Don't offer payment, as this only offends, but maybe leave a few dollars for food and bus fares.

108 Forming a babysitters club

Some parents save on babysitting costs by forming a loose collective of reciprocal babysitters. It usually works on a points system (so many points per hour before or after midnight) and seems like an excellent idea on paper. Just make sure you know your fellow club members very well. People change when they have children; perfectly sane friends can develop very odd attitudes when it comes to their children. My brother-in-law had an unpleasant experience—one club member requested that, being a man, he not be allowed to babysit her children alone. Needless to say, the club was abandoned shortly afterwards. However, if you can make it work without destroying friendships, it's a great way to save money.

109 Being afraid to employ babysitters

This is a symptom of the general paranoia that has developed about stranger danger. Obviously, you don't entrust your child to the care of strangers, but don't allow yourself to fall into the trap of believing your child won't 'settle' with anyone other than yourself. It's important for a child to develop relationships with other adults and it's equally important that you retain a sense of your own independence. You're simply making a very large rod for your own back. Maintaining a healthy relationship with your partner through some private time away from the kids is far more important in the long term for your child's happiness and wellbeing.

When you leave for the night, be firm. Your child will doubtless holler and cling on like a limpet, but remove yourself without fuss from the situation and let the babysitter deal with it—that's what you're paying them for. Soon the child will be distracted and begin to enjoy the novelty of someone new to play with; at worst, they'll cry themselves to sleep, which won't do them any harm in the long run. I certainly hope not.

Likewise, try to encourage your children to make use of kids'-club facilities on holidays, no matter how much they protest—they're too young for the aqua bar and anyway, who's paying for it?

10

THE EXTENDED FAMILY

'Wombat was delighted. "You lucky, lucky puss to have a nuncle. I haven't anyone. Is he a cat like you?"'
Ruth Park, The Muddle-headed Wombat

Use this page to record essential phone numbers: pizzeria, DVD shop and liquor outlet.

In days of yore, the concept of family was much wider than it is today. Grandparents, uncles (or nuncles), aunts, nieces, nephews, cousins and even the neighbours all joined together in the task of raising children. In and out of each other's houses, children scampering through the clouds of flour as Gran baked the morning's bread, kettle steaming lazily on the hob while dogs chased their tails underfoot and chickens clucked in the coop. Well, that's certainly how Milly-Molly-Mandy grew up and she seemed perfectly happy, despite having only one dress for summer and one dress for winter.

In today's hectic world, it's rare for the extended family to function as it once did, unless the daughter's been knocked up early and she, the sullen boyfriend and their unexpected joy are forced to move in with Mum and Dad because they can't pay rent anywhere else. More often than not, it's difficult for young families to be able to afford to buy a house in the suburb they grew up in, so families are separated much more than they once were. And aware of the pressures of their own family lives, we shy away from involving uncles and aunts;

often we don't know our neighbours well enough to entrust the cat to their care, let alone the kids; and grandparents are invariably off in a campervan or on a cruise through the Rhineland burning up the family inheritance.

110 Having children when your own parents are getting on a bit

If you have young children, there's nothing more pointless than their grandparents being decrepit. Let's face it, you've spent your whole life as a child selfishly demanding your parents' time and attention, so why should it stop when you have your own kids? There's a Japanese proverb that reads:

> When you have children yourself, you begin to understand what you owe your parents.

Lovely sentiment, but I say, 'Hold that thought'. There's plenty of time to repay the debt to Mater and Pater when they're no longer needed as babysitters on a Saturday night.

Older grandparents are a particular waste of space with toddlers. You can't send them down to the park as guardians when your three-year-old can easily outpace their motorised wheelchair. They have trouble lifting small people onto the monkey bars without risking expensive and ongoing chiropractic bills. In extreme cases, they have about as much idea of where they live as the child does. No, have your kids when you're young and your parents are still youthful enough to embarrass you with their taste in music. Live close—next door is handy—and if you can time starting a family for the first empty days of their retirement when they lack any purpose in life, perfect.

111 Relying on your parents' memories for child-rearing advice

When you're in the thick of dealing with a new baby, you have no idea of how quickly you'll eventually forget all of these problems and routines that you're now encountering on an daily basis. Having endured changing nappies for years, within months of being rid of them they'll be gone from your mind completely. Supermarket aisles of baby products that you haunted will become foreign and strange lands.

Similarly, your own parents will often have little or no memory of what to do with a new baby. Of course, we all retain an instinctive feel for handling small children, but the details get vague. Lacking today's meticulous medical records, their knowledge of the specific childhood diseases that you endured can be sketchy, often simply assuming that you had everything. During an outbreak of chickenpox, I was reassured by my mother that I'd had it as a boy, but the reverse was in fact the case, as I found out when I caught it from a pestilent child in the mothers' group. And while we're on the subject, Pinetarsol baths do little to ease the discomfort. It looks like you're soaking in your own urine and, for all the good it does, you might as well be.

112 Forgetting that how you treat your parents will influence the way your children treat you

Children learn by example, sadly, so how you relate to your parents and siblings will have an impact on their own behaviour. Remember that their little brains don't understand that your interplay is simply light-hearted banter and that Mummy muttering 'interfering and manipulative control freak' under her breath after Grandma has phoned is just play-acting. Treat your parents with love and respect and then maybe one day you too will be put in a nice home with bathroom facilities an easy walking-frame shuffle down the corridor.

113 Not taking advantage of the extended family

There can be a tendency in some young parents to want to go it alone, a desire to cement the new family unit by shutting off from the old. This is perfectly understandable and probably not a bad idea for a few days, one week tops. Bear in mind that you've got this new family for life; there's plenty of scope for 'just us' quality time down the track. And remember it's not so much a new family as an extension of the existing one. Exposure to the extended family builds your children's social skills and reduces their dependency on you, allowing you to get away every now and then, building to longer periods when you can have a few weeks in Thailand or something. Believe me, kids don't want to go to Florence; they'll be much happier staying with the cousins, especially if they have a pool.

114 Forgetting the extended family is a two-way street

If you send the kids to their auntie's for a sleepover, you've got to reciprocate, unwelcome as the thought of more children in the house might be. If you ask the neighbour to keep an eye on the kids for an hour, you'll have to do something in return. Not buy flowers or chocolates—it'd be cheaper to get a babysitter—but something neighbourly, like taking in their garbage bins or keeping them informed of interesting local-council developments. Maybe learn their first names and use them as required.

115 Heeding the advice of siblings with children

Just because one has children, it doesn't make one an expert. Sometimes siblings, particularly older ones, may feel a pressing need to advise you on how to bring up your child. The advice may be forthrightly offered, or delivered in a more subtle way: a disapproving look here, an indirect comment reported to another family member then relayed to you, or an anonymous letter in strangely recognisable handwriting left on your doorstep. My advice, as I advise in all matters of advice, is to graciously accept the advice and then decide whether to act on it later. For anyone in the advice business, the pleasure is in the giving; they're not all that interested in the outcome, it's simply that their opinion has been heard. To refuse or openly question advice is merely to be provocative and that can only lead to resentment. Simply say: 'That's interesting, I might give that a go'. You can then add: 'In a hundred years' under your breath as they drive away.

116 Ignoring the advice of siblings with children

Yes, it's the complete opposite of everything I just said, but that's the way with raising kids: black can just as easily be white. And yes, I've said that before but I have to repeat everything a hundred times before anyone will listen to me. Expediency is the name of the game and sometimes you can learn valuable lessons from those who have gone before. Look at the results of their parenting skills and determine what works and what doesn't. If you like your nieces and nephews, chances are the parents have done something right. It could be something as simple as enforcing a bedtime routine, or a more complex strategy like sending the child to boarding school from the age of five followed by compulsory military service.

Sharing a family history, your siblings can throw light onto puzzling aspects of your child's behaviour. 'Don't you remember? I always used to do that when I was his age.' Or 'That's where it comes from—you used to be just like that: completely uncoordinated!'

117 Disregarding the significance of genetics

As we discover more about the human genome, the age-old observation of family likenesses assumes a more scientific basis. However, we must distinguish between genetic and familial inheritance. A propensity to arthritis, say, is not a genetic trait, but it is familial. Other medical conditions are inherited genetically and the more you know about your family's medical history, the better prepared you are for what may lie ahead.

On a more general basis, it's also widely accepted that you will eventually turn into some form of your mother or father, however unsettling that may be. Complex as humans are, our essential nature has remained fairly consistent for thousands of years because we simply inherit our parents' characteristics, which is why we can read Shakespeare today and say: 'There's someone just like that at the office, except he's not a king'.

Personalities form in your children as the combination of family inheritance and the environment they live in. From personal experience—and this is not scientifically or statistically significant, based as it is on a sample of two—I'd suggest that a child is born pretty much as it intends to go on and little will change it.

If this book teaches you anything it is this:

Most of what you do as a parent is merely tinkering around the edges of a genetic blueprint that is intractable.

Twins illustrate this theory quite neatly. With the benefit of hindsight, their characters can be traced back to the womb; one will dominate, the other recede. Twin A, named at the first ultrasound, will forever try to lord it over Twin B. For the first year of their lives, our twin daughters slept in their cots as they had in the womb: one stretched out commandingly, the other curled in a tight ball as if trying to squeeze into the remaining space. Nine years later, they still do. So here's a tip for parents of multiples: whichever twin is born first, tell them they came out second.

118 Apportioning genetic characteristics to either side of the family

Funnily enough, all the good characteristics—politeness, creativity, sporting prowess etc.—will come from your partner's side of the family, and all the duds—bossiness, tendency to fat, bad temper and so on—will be traced through your genetic line. Confusingly, genetically inherited characteristics can skip generations; it may have been hundreds of years ago that your side of the family were the size of barges, but then, surprisingly, the trait reappears and you've got a couple of grunters on your hands. You may think that Junior's innate ability to play the tuba comes from your grandmother, little realising that your wife's family boasted a sousaphone specialist way back in the 1800s. Nature throws in the odd curve-ball, just to keep us guessing.

119 Letting the family birthdays slide

One of the trials of a growing extended family is the increasing number of birthday and Christmas gifts that have to be bought for various nephews and nieces. There is an eternal calendar on our fridge with birthdays of family and significant friends listed—honestly, I don't know why we don't just move to the gift shop permanently and save on the travel time. The list seems to keep growing. However, if you expect your kids to get any decent gifts from the family, you've got to put in the effort—you send a lousy five dollars in a card (preferably handmade) and that's what you'll get back.

120 Forgetting that not all young relatives will like each other

Obviously, you want your children to be welcomed in by all members of the family, but don't panic if they don't always get on with the nephews and nieces. One doesn't choose one's family. Relatives who live in close proximity have a better chance of forming closer relationships; those seen only at Christmas might struggle to have a decent conversation. Remember too that children can be surprisingly fickle; friendship is bartered about as easily as Pokémon cards as they build a sense of identity and discover who is truly like-minded among their peers.

ROLE MODELS FOR THE INEFFECTIVE PARENT

Number Two

THE DJUGASHVILIS (BETTER KNOWN AS THE STALINS)

Another of the world's great monsters you wouldn't have wanted in your playgroup was the communist dictator Joseph Stalin, an enigmatic tyrant responsible for the deaths of millions in the gulags and secret-police purges of Soviet Russia. Stalin presided over a regime of terror almost unmatched in history—ironically, it was the logical extension of a system of repression he had learned from his masters in the seminary school, a school his mother had struggled desperately to have him attend. Typical ineffective parent: you think you're doing the right thing and look where it leads you.

Stalin was born in Gori, Georgia, in 1878, in an impoverished shack that still stands today—perfect for the first-home buyer, a real fixer-upper if you can ignore the mausoleum that's been constructed around it and you don't mind increasingly decrepit tourists visiting to pay homage and remember the glory days of the USSR. Gori was then a violent, rough-and-tumble place where street brawling seems to have been organised on a semi-official basis. How things have changed in Georgia!

His father was a drunken cobbler called Beso Djugashvili. (Funnily enough, Adolf Hitler's father had early training in shoemaking and liked a drink as well. So if your dad runs a

Mister Minit franchise and doesn't mind a beer, watch out for latent signs in yourself of world domination.) His mother, Keke, was a serf who turned to the church for solace in a difficult life; her first two children having died, she invested all her emotional energy into Joseph, or 'Soso', as she nicknamed him. Ironic when you think about it, because what he did to the people of Russia was anything but so-so.

Despite becoming a violent alcoholic, Beso initially owned his small boot-making shop, which made him relatively well off. Says a lot about Gori. The family home was often filled with priests—some historians suggest that Stalin's father was in fact one of said priests and not Beso the shoemaker at all; others believe that to be a load of cobblers. However, it is true that one priest in particular dragged Beso down the path of drunkenness, sharing long and bitter drinking sessions throughout the night when he should have been damping his last or whatever it is that cobblers do.

Beso's increasing love of the bottle led to the Stalin family losing the shop and moving house nine times in the first ten years of Joseph's life, making it difficult for him to find and maintain friendships. Being unpleasant didn't help either. More significantly, the child became the victim of his father's progressively violent beatings. His mother fought to protect her son as best she could—in later years she would recount his love of the sweeter things in life: flowers, poetry and the systematic collectivisation of the means of production.

Young Stalin also appears to have been a bit accident prone—twice run over by horse-drawn vehicles, the legacy of which was a permanently damaged left arm that helped him avoid military service in World War I, and contracting

Role Models for the Ineffective Parent

smallpox at the age of seven, the facial scars haunting him for the rest of his life and making many a Kremlin photographer sweat as they tried to conceal them. He was also very short—160 centimetres, or 5 feet 4 inches in the bourgeois capitalist running-dog imperial scale, and in later life wore platform shoes to conceal it, anticipating disco fashion footwear by a good four decades. Stalin had another physical oddity: the second and third toes of his left foot were joined together, which may have enabled him to swim more quickly in a clockwise circle, although history doesn't reveal if he ever tried to.

He was, however, a very bright student and he was accepted into the local school, where he became quite the young poet. Unfortunately, Beso didn't share the family's enthusiasm for education, wanting his son to follow in the noble tradition of cobbling, and on hearing the news of Joseph's career plan, smashed half the windows in the town and attacked the local police chief. He abandoned the family shortly afterwards and moved elsewhere.

Stalin's good grades and his mother's love of the church and the priesthood (perhaps literally) ensured his entry into the seminary, where it was Keke's dream that he would study to become a priest. Joseph had other ideas, by all accounts becoming an atheist in his first year and turning instead to revolutionary literature, Russia at the time being a hotbed of anarchist and anti-tsarist thought. To counter such insurgent activity, the priests had an elaborate system of spies, informers and pre-emptive raids on the dormitories; Stalin apparently observed their activities and took copious notes. Years later, he made the brothers look like rank amateurs.

At one stage his father kidnapped him and took him off to the shoe factory in Tiflis, but young Stalin's sole wasn't in it. He was rescued by his mother and returned to school, although he increasingly turned to radical politics and was expelled in 1899 for not sitting his final exams. Even so, he was grateful to his mother for the rest of her life, installing her in a palace in Georgia, where she kept herself largely to one room and refused to believe any ill of her son, despite growing evidence to the contrary.

So what did the parents do wrong? Obviously, not everyone who has suffocating maternal love, paternal violence, poverty, alcoholism and overweening religion in their childhood becomes a communist dictator, although you can see the obvious attraction. As ways out go, it's up there. It is a mystery of behavioural science that some children endure the same environments and yet emerge as completely different adults, even within the same families. Maybe if Stalin's siblings had survived, his egocentricity would have been mollified; maybe if his father had joined Rotary instead of drinking himself to death, he might have pursued his childhood love of poetry with less triumphalism. If his mother had doted on him but given the seminary a miss, he might have become a hair stylist. Who knows?

11

THE INNER CHILD

'I have found the best way to give advice to your children is to find out what they want and then advise them to do it.'
Harry S Truman

Warning: this page does not absorb vomit.

Imagine how much easier life would be if you could read your child's mind. We struggle to work out what a crying baby is telling us—do you want more food? More sleep? We battle to decipher the significance of their first words—do you want more food? Less sleep? As they get a grip on the language, we fret over their silences or search for hidden meanings in their tentative phrases—what does 'I hate you, you are the worst parent ever!' exactly mean?

I'm reminded of the joke about the child who didn't speak a word until he was six. His anxious parents took him to every doctor and speech pathologist but could find nothing wrong with him. His first words, all those years later, were spoken at the breakfast table. 'This toast is cold', he said. His mother, astounded, asked why he had never spoken before. 'Because,' he replied, 'up until now everything has been perfectly satisfactory.'

My mother assures me I was equally easygoing, although I suspect she might be either biased or demented. Fat chance of such equanimity with the current generation. Convinced of the trauma that awaits them if we don't get it right—because after all, for the ineffective parent, if you're going to mess with anything at all it's going to be their heads—we anxiously try to read their mental condition and guide their impressionable minds towards a state of balance. If you don't sort out that the-soft-toys-are-coming-to-life nightmare now, you could have a heroin addict on your hands in fifteen years' time. You know who they'll be blaming when they're on the analyst's couch.

121 Trying to second-guess your child's emotional state

I've written elsewhere in this book that the modern parent is afraid of their children. In truth, it's more a case of being afraid of putting them into a bad mood. Painful as the experience may be for all concerned, children occasionally need to be reminded of their imperfections and trying to keep them in a state of perpetual contentment is not only impossible, it's counterproductive in the long term. You can't make life fabulous for them—they have to learn the hard way that life is not fair. What you can do is teach them the coping mechanisms to deal with the injustice of it all, and what safer place to do that than in the comfort of their own home?

122 Anticipating emotional difficulties

Don't misread the signs of your child's emotional state. As they learn how to respond to various stimuli, so too are they learning behavioural patterns to elicit a response from you. I'd go so far as to say that 75 per cent of a child's behaviour is purely for the benefit of its primary caregiver. Learn to recognise when the child is deliberately pushing your buttons.

Research has shown that this tends to be in their waking hours, although the truly skilled can have you on a string even when asleep.

123 Thinking too quickly that your child has a problem

Yes, some children have problems and they need help, but believe it or not, most children don't. As part of my extensive research for this book, I've read a lot of parenting books (alright—I've skimmed four) and if anything, I found that nearly everything I've thought of as a potential problem is remarkably common. So much so, that you'd have to say it constitutes normal behaviour. In our quest for 'perfect' children, we've been fooled into thinking that anything that doesn't fit into our perceptions of what we want our child to be is aberrant. Problems begin to exist simply because they've been labelled as being a problem. For example, when did a noisy, boisterous child with a short attention span cease to be just that and become a clinical problem that needs medication? Has the incidence of autism really exploded or are we labelling kids who in the past may have been described as vague, eccentric or reclusive?

Obviously, there are genuine cases of all these conditions and with greater reporting the diagnoses may have increased, but perhaps there's some other agenda at play. Define a problem and you can sell the solution. All of these 'problem' children are fuel for the burgeoning industry of counsellors, therapists, child psychologists and family mediators, not to mention the pharmaceutical companies. Perhaps in many cases a dose of common sense would be more useful than a dose of mood suppressants.

124 Denying your child has a problem

You see? Typically ineffective parent who can't make up his mind. Of course there's a flipside to the above: the denial, despite all evidence to the contrary, that your child's behaviour cannot be explained away as being highly individual. It's an awful admission for any parent to have to make, to realise your child has difficulties that make all the complaints in this book so trivial and indulgent. There but for the grace of God go I. Appraise your child dispassionately and without irrational fear and if you're worried, visit your GP.

125 Indoctrinating your child with your religious beliefs

Speaking of God, if religion were not taught to children it would cease to exist within two generations. If you're so sure of your beliefs, why not put them to the test and refrain from introducing them to your child until he or she is old enough to make a rational, measured assessment of their validity? That's what atheists do. I can find no proof or even suggestion of the existence of God, but I'm more than happy for my children to try and find it if they ever feel the need. Of course I can't prove that God *doesn't* exist, but I can't prove that the sun is not a giant hamster disguised in a star suit either.

126 Indulging the 'shy' child

My sister has always said to her children: 'There's no such thing as shy in this house'. At first, I thought it was a harsh thing to say, but I now see the wisdom in it. Almost as many parents think their child 'sensitive' as they believe them 'gifted and talented', but is anyone really born shy? Some kids are more reluctant to engage with the world than others,

The Inner Child

but the fact of the matter is they have to. Like so many other behavioural traits, shyness is as much learned as anything else. Sometimes, when indulged by an over-protective parent, it's worn as a badge of honour and becomes a self-fulfilling prophecy. There's a lot to be said for behavioural positivism; I'm not sure if such a thing exists, but if it doesn't it jolly well should.

Of course, the child who has difficulty socialising or is physically overawed by the wider world needs help to overcome timidity, but constantly hearing role models saying 'Oh, she's just shy' is really no help at all.

127 Treating your children as small adults

They're not—they're children. I'm not sure where this modish obsession with treating children as equals came from, but it flies in the face of all science and logic. Respect and protect them by all means, but don't expect them to behave in the same way as you do. Perhaps it's a backlash against the perception that childhood is an invention of the Victorian age and consequently to be dismissed as old-fashioned. Of course, we don't want them to be chimney sweeps or working in a coal mine at the age of nine, or married to the King of Spain when they're thirteen. We don't want a return to childhood ending abruptly as soon as they're capable of labour and we rail against the exploitation of children in the developing world, yet at the same time we seem intent on making our children grow up as quickly as possible. How else can one explain Bratz dolls and the emergence of the tweeny market?

Childishness in adults is rightly frowned upon, but ideally it should be encouraged in children. It's what they do best.

Why prematurely rob them of a belief in Santa Claus when there is as much evidence to suggest he exists as there is to support the otherworldliness of the Dalai Lama or God? They have a lifetime to not believe in the tooth fairy, so why not give them ten years' grace?

One often hears: 'But children are exposed to so much more these days—the average ten-year-old knows much more than I ever did'. That may well be so, but it doesn't mean he understands it. Being exposed to an adult world doesn't ipso facto make you an adult. The ability of a child to negotiate with the world and the speed of the development of their psychological, intellectual and physical being hasn't changed radically, despite the hormones in chicken. Their brains continue to develop in ways we don't readily appreciate. Prosaic truths like an inability to judge the speed of approaching vehicles in their peripheral vision until they're twelve is a good reason to keep walking them to school, rather than saying, 'Oh well, you can operate the hard-drive recorder without the manual; of course you're old enough to walk there by yourself'.

Far better if we, as the supposedly more mature and insightful beings, try to see the world through their eyes instead of insisting that they look at it through ours.

128 Not allowing your children to be bored

Given the hectic schedule of activities that so many children subscribe to, I'm amazed they have time to breathe. I remember long periods of boredom as a child—I remember long periods of boredom yesterday—but I never felt a pressing need to fill them with jazz ballet, touch football or figure skating. There's nothing wrong with them being at a loose end; it might motivate them to create something. If necessity is the mother of invention, surely boredom is the father. Don't feel obliged to serve up endless distractions on a plate.

129 Not loving your child the same way when they're awake as you do when they're asleep

Nothing can prepare you for the intensity of feeling when you gaze at your sleeping child. If you were called upon to sacrifice your life for them, it would be a lot easier if you could get them to fall asleep and look adorable before you threw yourself in front of the speeding bus, marauding home invader or whatever. Awake, they're a different ball game altogether.

Look, everyone knows how hard it is to love a child sometimes—the whingeing child, the nagging child, the surly, sullen, difficult, rude, ungrateful, over-tired, tantrum-throwing, disrespectful, fighting, jealous child. Unfortunately, when a child is being at her most difficult and unpleasant, that's often the time when she needs your love most. Never reward bad behaviour, but don't think of your love as a reward in itself; love should be the default position, no matter what your child does. Within limits, of course. If they trash the house, all bets are off.

130 Allowing your child to become materialistic

I heard a mother complain that she couldn't get her son out of a shop without buying him something. Here's a plan: you just walk out and I promise you he will follow. Still, I know the feeling—we can't go to the zoo without buying a soft toy. It's worse when we take the kids with us. Children are increasingly being targeted by marketing experts—through their parents in the early years and then, as they acquire discretionary spending power (formerly known as pocket money), by a direct barrage of advertising, peer-group pressure and an omnipresent retail industry. Resist it at all costs. On the bright side, the world will probably be ruined in the next twenty years, what with climate change and all, so they won't be able to get to the shops quite as much.

131 Not teaching your children the value of waiting

In this age of instant gratification, it's ironic that the more we're gratified, the less satisfied we become. Teach your children the value of patience; anticipation makes the reward all the more delicious. Think how much they'll enjoy that puppy if they have to wait until they're eighteen to get it.

12
TWINS AND MULTIPLES

'Having one child makes you a parent; having two,
you are a referee.'
David Frost

Even if you're not a parent of multiple-born children, read this chapter because you'll feel much better—you think you've got problems? Now's your time for a bit of *schadenfreude*, a German word meaning happiness at the misfortune of others. Which, when you think about it, is pretty much as German as you can get. The inept raising of twins is a subject on which I can actually speak with some authority, having been blessed—and I use the word advisedly—with twin daughters in 2000. Their arrival in the millennial year certainly marked a seismic shift in our modest corner of the earth and it's been a downhill slide ever since. No, I'm only joking—it's actually been dreadful. Even the singleton firstborn will change your life forever; having twins transforms your world and then rubs your nose in it.

I wish I had a dollar for every time I've heard: 'Instant family, got it all over at once, hey?' or 'Double the trouble but twice the fun!' Still, not as inane as the question posed to the father of a girl-boy pairing: 'Are they identical?' (Although funnily enough, identical twins can, in very rare circumstances, be of different genders. Something to do with a dropped X chromosome at the time of the cleavage of the egg—whatever that is; I always thought it was something to do with omelettes.) I can only begin to imagine what it would be like to have triplets or even more. My advice to anyone finding themselves in that scenario would be to find a country with no extradition treaty or do the honourable thing and retire to the study with a revolver.

Twins are particularly difficult if they're your first children. I'm sure with one or two under your belt, the arrival of two more at the same time could be optimistically regarded as more of a mild inconvenience than a problem. For the inexperienced parent, however, the workload is not doubled, it's squared. Feeding, cleaning and sleeping have to be co-ordinated, your local council eventually refuses to take away the huge piles of used nappies, and you quickly discover that no twin pram is designed to fit through a standard door. Getting out and about becomes more difficult, and it's hard to safely wrangle two active toddlers simultaneously, particularly for the more mature parent.

And speaking of maturity, increased age is an important factor in the incidence of twin births—the older you are, the more likely you are to have twins. Other factors include family history, increased intake of folic acid (often used as a preventative measure if there is a history of spinal birth defects in the family) and the rising incidence of IVF treatments. Oddly enough, some studies suggest that taller women are more likely to have twins and Nigerian women of the Yoruba tribe with a diet high in yams will have multiple births more often. Apparently, if they ease up on the yams, the twin rate drops. No studies have yet been done on what happens if they switch to a diet of Italian food or yam-replacement energy drinks.

Still, the rewards are many, despite the many pitfalls:

132 Allowing twin babies to feed at will

There's a particular parenting philosophy that suggests you feed your child at will and let them sleep whenever and wherever they want. This is a simple recipe for insanity for anyone but particularly the parents of multiples. Routine, always important in a baby's life, is essential for the smooth running of a multiples household. Breastfeeding can be difficult with two; for some reason one on each available outlet doesn't seem to work as well as it should, but try and feed as close together as possible. Bottles, despite their bad press, do make the job easier and allow helpers to share the load. In fact, twins demand a greater degree of help all round, particularly from Dad.

133 Allowing twins to sleep when they want to

Knock that on the head as soon as possible. If the twins don't fall asleep together, adopt this simple strategy: as soon as one drops off, drug the other one. No, all jokes aside—it's worth a shot. Actually, synchronised sleeping for two is no more difficult to achieve than settling an active singleton down for the night; i.e. all but impossible. Darken the room with lead-lined windows, alert visitors with a cheeky, hand-drawn sign that future prime ministers are sleeping, and try to catch a nap while the kids do. It's amazing what six and a half minutes of unbroken sleep can do for you.

134 Seeing them as two halves of a whole

Up to a very small point that's a valid observation, but remember they are two separate human beings. Try to avoid buying them the same toys, cots, books and, later in life, the same computers, cars etc.—and they'd probably prefer separate apartments as well, or at least a duplex. Obviously, to avoid argument—and studies show that twins fight more often and intensely than singleton siblings—it's tempting to give each twin exactly the same but don't. You are simply making two rods for your own back.

135 Saying 'And the other half's for you'

I read a survey of things twins most disliked and other than 'our parents', the despair on being told 'And the other half's for you' struck a chord. Why shouldn't a twin be given something whole and entire for itself? Buddhist monks aside, none of us really like sharing. It's something we learn to do but, like so many ethical and moral choices, it has to be drilled into us. Witness the only child confronted by the arrival of a baby brother or sister. Life, which up to that point had been going swimmingly, suddenly becomes about compromise and negotiation. Twins don't even get that brief period in the sun, those blessed years of the singleton's parental full attention when he or she alone is the centre of the universe. Twins have to operate in a two-sun galaxy; triplets in a three-sun; quadruplets in a … I think you get my point.

136 Trying too hard to be 'fair'

The sooner you can instil in them the idea that they won't always get the same things in life, the better. As soon as twins learn the power of envy and jealousy, they can make lives hell for their parents—one gift is always seen as better than the other, and so on. But life will not be fair to them; a callous world won't recognise the equal entitlement of their twindom, so prepare them for life's harsh realities. Give one the genuine article, the other a cheap imitation; one gets porridge, the other gruel. Mix it up and keep them guessing, just like life.

137 Dressing twins identically

Although this can be good for a laugh when people have no idea which twin they're talking to, it's not helpful in the development of their individual identities. Ditto being referred to as 'the twins', although perversely, most twins are quite proud of their status and don't mind it half as much as their parents and child psychologists do. In fact, many twins, even fraternal ones, will choose to dress alike of their own accord. In this case, when in their company, attach a small placard to yourself saying 'I didn't dress them like that'. If the twins are a boy-girl combination and insist on dressing alike, seek professional help.

Having said that, being dressed identically can be a useful way to identify them in a crowd. There can't be many people wearing the same striped jumpsuit and brightly coloured sunhat, especially when they're thirteen.

And here's a tip: twins are a particularly appealing novelty for people of Asian cultures, being comparatively rare in those countries (almost non-existent in Japan)—the Chinese consider them lucky. On holidays in China, you can make the children busk or simply park their pram on a busy street with a hat in front of it.

138 Not separating twins at school

There are differing levels of co-dependency with twins that tend to run in this fashion from highest to lowest:

1. Identical girls
2. Fraternal girls
3. Identical boys
4. Fraternal boys
5. Mixed pair: girl-boy
6. Mixed pair: boy-girl

The last category is statistically meaningless.

Some twins will want to stay together at school; others will benefit from being in different classes; some thrive in completely different schools. That's probably going too far, what with all the driving and running about you'll have to do and it's bad enough going to the meetings of one parent-teacher committee, let alone two. You may find that your local school has a policy on how to place multiples. Listen carefully to the teachers and, indeed, your twins' wishes, then simply ignore them all and do whatever's most convenient for you.

My advice is to let your twins begin their educational journey together in kindergarten, then split them into separate classes to avoid competition—they get more than enough of that at home. Encourage them to develop separate friends and interests. Have one learn French, the other German, so they're more use on European holidays. (Chinese holidays: see habit 137.)

139 Telling your twins which one was born first

We all expect the oldest child in a family to be dominant and demanding—being the youngest in my family, I know that for a fact. But it's surprising to find that being even a few minutes older can have exactly the same effect. In these days of ultrasounds and in-uterine imaging, dominant twins are identified in the womb and labelled as Twin A. It usually follows that they're the firstborn. However, how much of the dominance they then go on to exercise is the result of knowing they were first out?

Our twins were delivered (like many) by caesarean section, so in a sense they both saw daylight simultaneously—my wife could see them lying side by side reflected in the obstetrician's face mask. I was too preoccupied—in a supine position being revived by medical staff; I've never taken well to a procedure—to pay close attention, but technically, Twin A was removed first; Twin B followed less than a minute later. Our mistake was to tell them that, so now any dispute about rank, precedence, priority, position, title or even who gets to sit in the front seat of the car is capped by 'Well, I'm the oldest' just seconds before the first punch lands.

Much better to leave the child confused, feeling strangely superior yet believing that she's not the oldest. Undoubtedly, with the instinctive cunning of the firstborn, she will play the 'I'm the youngest' card with equally devastating effect.

140 Comparing twins with each other

A bad idea with any of your children but difficult to resist when you're living with a potentially interesting genetic-sociological experiment. Twins behave differently to other siblings, even those born close together. Sometimes they'll define themselves by what the other is not and can often take a complimentary behavioural role that shifts backwards and forwards between them over time. At its most simple, this manifests itself as the evil twin–good twin dichotomy. One will be helpful when the other is being difficult; one will reach a developmental milestone while the other struggles. But be reassured, it all evens out in the wash, even if the advanced one ends up going backwards. The child's true nature will only be revealed in the absence of their other half, in much the same way that any child's personality is best observed in the absence of their parents.

141 Having a favourite

This is a dilemma that haunts all parents, with multiples or not. Obviously, one child is going to be more appealing than the others—I know I'm the favourite in my family, despite what my sisters say. It might, however, be best to keep your cards close to your chest; apparently, it's psychologically damaging to *not* be the favourite. On the other hand, some behaviour specialists believe it's equally damaging to believe you are the family's chosen one because it will lower your self-reliance and independence. With twins, being so close and easily comparable, favouritism can be more of a delicate issue although thankfully, given the yin-and-yang nature of the relationship, you'll find your affections waver as each passes through a phase.

142 Feeling guilty for having a favourite

Don't lose another minute's sleep on this one. On the plus side, favouritism can be a useful disciplinary tool—use it as a bargaining chip for good behaviour, viz: 'You won't be the favourite any more if you don't make your bed and put that towel back on the rack'. Or: 'Your sister thinks she's the favourite, but if you do your homework, it could easily be you'.

I'm sure picking a favourite has an evolutionary function. If you pick the right one, your extra encouragement and attention will further its success in life; if you back the dud, at least the increased love and devotion will help bring it up to speed. And ask yourself this: am I really selecting a favourite or just enjoying the company of this particular child at this particular moment? Who knows what tomorrow will bring?

143 Aligning one child with one parent

We've all heard the expressions 'She's a real daddy's girl' or 'He's mum's boy, alright', but be wary of aligning one twin with one parent. If you're not careful, Dad will always find himself stuck with one, Mum with the other. Perhaps introduce a lottery system to allocate quality time, although be sensitive in what you call it—no-one wants to be referred to as the Short Straw. And it's especially galling when your kids start using it to refer to you.

144 Believing your twins have a secret language

It's sometimes thought that twins communicate via a language known only to them—the phenomenon has been given a scientific name, idioglossia or cryptophasia, so obviously there must be something in it. Probably not a great deal, however, because while there will occasionally be a case of identical twins devising a patois that only they understand, most secret twin languages turn out to be more a result of delayed speech development than anything else. Twins, on average, acquire speech more slowly than singletons, possibly because they don't receive the same amount of individual attention, are not spoken to directly as often and reinforce each other's speech patterns and mistakes. Therefore, the secret languages are usually, on closer inspection, immature attempts with repeated errors. Not unlike many adults' attempts at public speaking.

145 Inviting playmates over one at a time

I know I've been banging on about individuality, but it's probably best to encourage your twins to pursue their individual friendships off-site. Away from the family home, they're much more pleasant—another reality check for any parent: children usually display their worst behaviour in the family home. When one twin brings home a friend, the resultant three-way tensions invariably end in disaster. Triangles are inherently unstable, so why not invite a friend over for the other twin as well? Then the ensuing bunfight is much better balanced.

146 Discouraging individual sleepovers

Twins are often regarded as being inseparable and consequently their friends (and more particularly their friends' parents) may be reluctant to invite one over without the other. Make sure you let the parental network know that it's better for the twins to have some time apart and that individual sleepovers are welcome for a night, or better still, a few weeks. Encourage each of your twins to cope without the other. This is much easier in a boy-girl pairing—your boy probably won't be interested in an invitation to a Barbie-themed sleepover! On the other hand, he may be flattered—maybe even a little curious.

Use this page to make a list of the lists you have to make.

13
THE TOP TEN

Use this page to prioritise the list you made of the lists you have to make.

Time poor with the endless demands of a busy family? Can't be bothered to read the whole book and need a quick-fix solution for your disastrous attempts at parenting? Lost the ability to concentrate for more than five minutes?

What?

Well, they may not be the *top* Top Ten, but everything about being a parent is compromise. Consider that the eleventh. So, here they are in one convenient list for you to cut out and stick on the fridge.

147 Sticking things on the fridge

Alright, maybe not in the top ten but a neat segue, you'd have to admit. And quite seriously, you think you're organised and smart with your fridge-door layout—emergency numbers listed alphabetically; Leunig or Far Side cartoon illustrating a 'life's like that' moment; postcards from exotic places being visited by friends without children; gas mark to centigrade oven converter handy for when you're cooking all those fabulous meals from the family cookbooks you've bought but never opened, and the program for the retro cinema that runs classics you just *have* to see, like *Rabbit-Proof Fence, Koyaanisqatsi* and the Italian remake of *Revenge of the Nerds.*

But before long your fridge is so covered with feeble artworks, canteen rosters, ballet class times, doctor's appointments, school newsletters, health warnings and counselling hotlines, it looks like a bomb's gone off in a stationery shop and your life disintegrates into the disorganised chaos your mother always warned you of because now you have no idea of when, where or why anything is happening.

And now, the real Top Ten:

1   Worrying about being a bad parent

Apart from those people who abuse or neglect their children, I don't think there is such a thing as a good or a bad parent. Almost every parent tries as best they can to master the inexact science of raising their children and just because some may be luckier and have an easier time of it than others, that doesn't necessarily make them 'better' parents. The greatest danger we face as modern parents is that we'll worry so much about the job we're doing, we'll forget why we're doing it in the first place. Worried parents perceive dangers where none lurk. Worried parents convey their own uncertainties and anxieties to their children. Sometimes as we struggle to give our children what we think we didn't have as a child, we lose sight of what we did.

2   Forgetting your children aren't made of glass

(This was advice given to us by my late Uncle Jimmy and, hard as it is to believe in the small hours of the morning when their breathing sounds funny, it's absolutely true. It's the first piece of advice that I give any new parent who hasn't asked for any.)

The curse of the modern parent's life: obsessive worry about their offspring. The longer the life expectancy of human beings becomes, the more ways we discover to potentially shorten it! No wonder we endlessly fret about our kids—we're bombarded daily with a litany of the disasters that may befall them. Don't succumb to the terror campaign and allow molehills to become mountains. A grazed knee is not a reason to have a day off preschool. An old dero flashing himself in the local park is not going to sexually traumatise anyone for life. A reluctance to do jigsaw puzzles does not signify attention deficit disorder. Riding a scooter without helmet, knee pads and elbow guards will not necessarily result in death. Not all camp sites are infested with snakes, spiders and falling tree limbs. Wearing a singlet will not stave off the common cold—nor is the common cold a reason for a doctor's visit and/or hospitalisation. As they say in the classics, don't fret the small stuff. But do get any odd-looking moles checked.

3   Thinking you should be your child's best friend

You shouldn't—you're his parent. Ideally, you'll like him and he'll like you in return, but a friend fulfils a very different function to a parent. A good friend can be non-judgemental; try as hard as you might, parents find it almost impossible to be so. And nor should you be. Your role is to essentially civilise the untamed, though admittedly small and relatively helpless, barbarian that is entrusted to your care. Hard decisions have to be made, even if they may be ultimately ignored. A whole lifetime of emotional baggage and neuroses has to be handed on to the next generation. Don't forget that, from a child's point of view, emotional attachment to a parent generally follows a U shape: intense to begin with, then diminishing, gradually increasing again, before rapidly growing as they realise you're about to render them an orphan. (And let me tell you, ungrateful child, it's a very good friend indeed who'll wipe your backside or clean up your vomit at three in the morning.)

4   Teaching your children rights but not responsibilities

We hear an awful lot about children's rights these days and like any other perceived benefit that might make their lives easier, children have been quick to make the most of them. It's unsettling to hear a five-year-old say: 'You can't talk to me like that; I've got rights'. Even when unable to point to any international protocol that specifically grants them such amnesty, today's child will vigorously fend off many attempts at discipline from a parent as a violation of their 'rights'. Regrettably, they have little grasp of the reciprocal notion of responsibilities.

Beyond the laws of basic human decency that extend to all people, children confuse rights with privileges. Nintendo is not a right; playing in the garden is not a right; being told you're marvellous is not a right. Teach your child that, as for anyone, privileges are the reward for carrying out their responsibilities. What those responsibilities are is up to you, but my advice would be start small and don't expect any miracles.

5 Doing anything for your child that she can do for herself

How often have you done something for your child simply because you know it will be easier and quicker to do it yourself? Personally, I've lost count. Given the time constraints of modern life—how naïve we were to think that computers and labour-saving devices would give us more 'leisure time'!—it's understandable that, mindful of the potential mess, you'll pour the milk for a small child, or pick up the dirty clothes because you can't bear to hear your own voice asking them to do it for the hundredth time. Children know this; they are expert manipulators. Cunning is an evolutionary trait that gives them a better chance of survival and believe me, it's one of the first things they learn.

Encourage your child to do things for himself as soon as he becomes capable. By doing they learn. Don't buy shoes with Velcro straps—tying shoelaces can lead to a love of knots and a potential career as a scout or tall-ship sailor. Advanced bed-making is a skill in high demand in the hospitality industries. Picking up towels must have some sort of value in later life.

6 Not teaching your child manners

There's a school of thought, popular with your post-modernists and cultural relativists, that manners aren't so important any more and are simply a codified pattern of behaviour designed to perpetuate an existing social power structure. With all respect (and pardon my French): crap. Your number one task as a parent is to equip your child to cope in the world and to give them the skills to lead a happy and fulfilled life as easily as they can. Manners and civility are the lubricant that keeps human society functioning and any child who has an understanding of how to relate to others in an amenable and respectful way will find life a hell of a lot easier to get through. I'm not talking about etiquette: teach your child the tenet of treating others in the way they themselves would like to be treated. Jesus and Mary Poppins were on to a good thing there.

7   Thinking that doing things for your child is the same as doing things with them

Some wise person said that the greatest gift you can give your children is your time. How true, although if you give them too much time you might all be spending it on the dole living in a dumpster. Some other wise person (there's a surprising number of them around) also said that a child will remember you playing a game with them but will never remember the shirt you ironed for them or the pristine bathroom you scrubbed. (On the other hand, they might remember bathing in mould or wearing the same shirt three weeks in a row.) Even so, it is a question of balance. Don't confuse the endless slog of doing things to *your* satisfaction with preparing the best outcome for your child. They'll probably be happier with a little less attention to domestic detail and a bit more fun on the floor.

8   Thinking that self-esteem should be given, not earned

You can't give a child a sense of self-worth—you have to give the child the willingness and ability to earn it. Endlessly telling a child that what he or she has done is fantastic will simply give them a sense of self-entitlement, not self-esteem. How can a child learn the relative merit and value of anything in life if they're given a blanket assurance that everything they do is great? If they paint a picture in five minutes and get told it's a masterpiece, why would they bother taking ten minutes to paint the next one? If they're equally rewarded for coming last, why would they ever strive to come fifth or, heaven forbid, first?

Self-esteem comes from the realisation of what you as a unique individual can offer to the world. If you begin life thinking you're good at everything, the eventual awakening to reality will be an especially rude one. Far better to equip your child to cope with inevitable failure and give them the resilience to keep searching for what makes them special.

9   Allowing your child to dictate your life

Obviously, having a child is going to alter your life dramatically and many allowances will have to be made to cater to their needs, but don't let the children dictate the terms of your life. One of the more alarming trends is the emergence of children into the foreground of daily life. In the past, children were very much a background feature; their parents continued to lead their own lives and the kids tagged along. It seemed to work perfectly well—ask yourself this: was I more or less satisfied with my childhood? Most people, if they're being honest, will probably answer yes, albeit with a few grumbles and minor qualifications.

But now our lives are dominated by our children, almost to the point where we've become scared of them—we worry about offending them, scarring them for life, depriving them, or in some way inadequately preparing them for the adult world. Why this cultural shift, particularly at a time when we've got more (materially, at any rate) to offer them than ever before? I suspect it has something to do with children being identified as a potential market; the power balance has been altered by the arrival of the child-as-consumer. Market pressure is being brought to bear on us as parents to buy more and do more for our children and if we don't, we feel inadequate.

My advice is to emulate the safety instructions given for the oxygen masks on an aeroplane: lead your own life first and tend to children when you've got that working. If you feel fulfilled and productive, your children can only learn by your example.

10 Not being what you want your children to be

I don't mean you have to be a highly paid orthopaedic surgeon or a supermodel. If you want your child to be honest, so too must you be. If you want your child to become a caring, loving and independent person then you'll have to lead by example. If you don't want your child to grow into a workaholic who sees little of her children, schedule half an hour of quality 'us' time, preferably each day.

14

THE ACTIVE CHILD

The Camel's hump is an ugly lump
Which well you may see at the Zoo;
But uglier yet is the hump we get
From having too little to do.

Kiddies and grown-ups too-oo-oo,
If we haven't enough to do-oo-oo,
We get the hump—
Cameelious hump—
The hump that is black and blue!

The cure for this ill is not to sit still,
Or frowst with a book by the fire;
But to take a large hoe and a shovel also,
And dig till you gently perspire …
Rudyard Kipling, 'How the Camel Got His Hump', Just So Stories

This page can be boiled as a low-fat, high-fibre snack.

Physical activity is a must for any child. It promotes healthy growth, coordination, flexibility, muscle strength, lung capacity and bodily confidence. However, it can also be a complete pain in the arse for any parent who has to spend an eternity in parks and playgrounds monitoring their offspring's physical prowess, standing about like meerkats on the alert for passing paedophiles. Ditto the endless weekend trips to sporting venues for soccer matches, netball games and athletics carnivals.

But I'm afraid you have to do it. Anyone can see that childhood obesity is on the rise; walk down any street and the number of small tubsters you see waddling along is alarming. There is no-one to blame for a child running to fat but the parents. Please don't tell me about 'glands'—that particular condition is very rare—and even being 'large-framed' only goes so far. No, it's a poor diet and little or no physical activity that sets a child on the road to stretch pants and a loose, oversized shirt, and as an ineffective parent, it's up to you to lift your game.

148 Not setting a good example in the fitness stakes

As noted elsewhere in this book when I was running short of ideas, children learn best by example and they learn most from the example set by their parents or significant caregivers. If your idea of exercise is walking to the car or playing ten minutes of tennis on a Wii console, odds on your child will regard physical activity as a pointless intrusion on quality lounge time. Set yourself a simple but effective exercise regime, even if it's just a walk around the neighbourhood, and encourage your child to come along. Drag them along if necessary—if nothing else, the extra weight will give you an increased aerobic workout. But seriously, exercise taken as a family can be very effective. Perhaps you could form a track relay team, even though it may be difficult to find an age category to compete in. Hunt down local fetes that encourage family participation in novelty sports, although personally I've always found sack racing to be slightly demeaning. Still, nothing like a three-legged race or a tug of war to provide a few minutes of family bonding, followed by bitter recriminations about who wasn't fast enough or pulling as if they meant it.

149 Avoiding the local park

There can be any number of good reasons for steering clear of the local park: dubious toilet blocks, unpleasant dogs and their unpleasant habits, yobs playing touch football, joggers, drug addicts, alcoholics, homeless people, insects, relentless sun, no shade, run-down play equipment, syringes, broken bubblers, swooping birds and mind-numbing tedium. Makes you wonder what they spend your bloody rates on.

Anyway, ignore all that. The park offers a cheap and handy facility for your child to run freely, to break out of the confines of the house and to explore the physical limitations and possibilities of his or her growing body. In a healthy, Outward Bound kind of way. Bad moods disappear once you get them out of the house (alright, briefly) and a combination of fresh air and exercise tires them out, ensuring a good night's sleep.

150 Steering clear of the play equipment

Do try to use the play equipment creatively. There's nothing worse than the sight of a distracted parent pushing a swing in a half-hearted, desultory fashion, particularly if there's no-one on it. That swing could be a launching pad for space adventure, although do take care of your lower back as you heave them back for lift-off, especially if this is the first step on a larger child's weight-loss journey. The swing bridge could have an evil troll lurking underneath—no prizes for guessing who'll be playing evil troll for the next three hours. The sliding pole could be in a fire station and you've got to answer the emergency call, especially if someone in your playgroup has actually set fire to the garbage bin or the windbreak of native plants put in by local Landcare volunteers.

For my money, an old-fashioned playground offers far more opportunities for creative and exhilarating play, but they're becoming harder to find. In my childhood, captured German artillery pieces from the Somme were still considered the thing for playground equipment, barrels plugged with cement and covered in a two-inch layer of lead-based paint. These were set in a dust bowl and surrounded by concrete, asphalt and anything else rock-hard that council could lay their hands on. Trees were cut back to the roots to ensure maximum exposure to the health-giving sun.

Modern playgrounds, erected by paranoid councils in constant fear of being sued, are either tame and benign collections of what look to be wooden pirate boats designed by Picasso in his cubist phase, or stark, minimalist sculptural affairs straight from Sweden called Plåygrønd, floating on a sea of foam rubber so children can bounce safely off the ground as they fall from the geometric climbing frame, or Tactile Responsive Mobility Unit. That's all well and good, but are they missing out on that life-affirming experience of danger confronted and narrowly avoided? That bittersweet moment as you fall off the mothballed howitzer and arc face first toward the cut glass embedded in cement to discourage the pigeons, realising that this is definitely going to need a tetanus booster, possibly stitches?

Find a playground that offers the best of both worlds. A roundabout that can still threaten injury if used unwisely, swings on long chains that can really fly and a seesaw that lands with a decent vertebrae-jarring thump. Then they can recover on the Pirät Bycet or spend some quiet time in the Élff Cäve playing shops.

151 Wrapping your child in cotton wool

So fearful is the modern parent of their child being hurt in any way that the traditional joys of childhood are being threatened. This obsession with physical safety has reached the absurd level of cartwheeling being banned in a Queensland primary school. How can you ban cartwheeling? Every healthy girl between the ages of seven and ten at some stage feels a compulsive need to cartwheel every fifteen seconds. The school insisted it was responding to a threat of litigation from the parents of a child injured in the playground while cartwheeling. Honestly, the teachers could form a protective ring around a child and shepherd him from one end of the playground to the other, but he's still going to fall over and scrape a knee.

This type of parent has a name: Belinda Stevenson, and she's a complete pain in the arse. No, I'm kidding—honestly, Belinda—they're the 'helicopter parent', so called for their tendency to hover over a child and drop in for rescue at the first sign of any danger, imagined or otherwise. Much better for the child to learn the limits of her physical capabilities, to recognise and analyse risks or dangers as they present themselves and to learn how to cope when accidents inevitably occur.

This sort of over-protectiveness manifests itself in:

152 Not giving a child a bike or scooter

I wasn't allowed a bike until I was thirteen—every other child got one as soon as they could sit on the seat. That denial, on the basis that it was too dangerous, has left me emotionally scarred for life. A timid child at the best of times—I think physical coward may be a more accurate description—it has taken me years to overcome my subsequent risk aversion. Even now, you couldn't pay me enough to go on a bungee jump and if a dog suddenly leaps up behind a gate and barks it takes me weeks to recover. Mind you, the dog phobia may be connected to the bike riding as I was constantly barked at when I eventually assumed the saddle.

Be that as it may, the point is don't deny your child the liberating freedom of a bicycle or scooter. I'm not suggesting that you send them out riding on the freeway, but with some care, a young child can enjoy the excitement and exercise two wheels can bring. If affordability is an issue, check on eBay a few weeks after Christmas because there'll be hundreds of them. Simply purchase, wipe off the blood and attach the trainer wheels.

153 Insisting on plastic scissors until the teen years

154 Banning glitter as an inhalation hazard

155 Assuming everything is toxic

156 Not letting your child do gymnastics

This is the cartwheeling phobia gone full circle, as it were. For young girls especially, gymnastics is right up there with horses, fairies and Nintendos. After each Olympic Games, there is a spike in the number of small people enrolling in rhythmic gymnastics. Ribbon and hoop sales go through the roof. Admittedly, competitive gymnastics involves years of intense training and twisting the infant body into unnatural shapes that leaves the child deformed for life, but think of the dough you could make if the kid does well. The trick is judging whether they've got what it takes before the incipient osteoporosis kicks in. And the ability to keep smiling despite having just shattered your collarbone in the dismount is a useful life skill.

The Active Child

157 Not letting your child in the surf

Is there anything sadder than a child in full sunsuit, hat and sunscreen sitting in a shade tent underneath a tree not allowed to venture across the sand into the water because the waves are a bit big? Teach your child to swim as soon as possible and throw them in. Statistically, the benign backyard pool poses a far greater threat than the beach.

158 Not letting your child play rugby league

While I realise having people who can read (i.e. you) associated with the game of rugby league can only help raise the standard and although I know that denying your youngster the chance to play full-contact ball sports is un-Australian, I actually think you've made the right call here. (Unless, of course, you want your child to embark on a life of drinking binges and group sex.) Ditto with not letting them join the cheerleaders. But here's an interesting strategy to foster self-reliance and resilience: have your son join the cheerleading squad and put your daughter in at half-back. (See Competitive Sport at the end of this chapter.)

159 Avoiding the study of martial arts

While not wishing to encourage violence in anyone, a martial art, particularly the more benign forms like taekwondo and extreme origami, can be a useful skill for a child to master. Self-defence of some sort can come in handy, although I have always found a decent sprint to be the best way to extricate oneself from any threatening situation. Strictly speaking, students of a martial art are forbidden by the code of honour from using the discipline outside the 'dojo' (Japanese for 'school hall out of hours'). But under extreme provocation, a nine-year-old is entitled to use the secret lore to defend himself. Don't allow your child to become too skilled—I'm reminded of the comedian Red Skelton's advice to parents: 'Never raise your hand to a child; it leaves your groin unprotected'.

160 Forbidding your child to go on school camp

Leaving the safety of the family home for three nights in a dorm with classmates, the days filled with alarming activities like abseiling, archery and white-water rafting, can be a challenging time for parents and children alike, particularly if you haven't done extensive police background checks on the teaching staff. Believe me, the experience of school camp, no matter how good or bad, will be character building for your child. You also get out of making school lunches for three days. School camp is a rite of passage, an assertion of independence and, like so many of the activities covered in this chapter, a building block in that most essential of qualities, resilience. The self-reliant child is a wonderful thing to behold and although you may wish to cling onto mutual need, you're not serving your child's best interest.

161 Forbidding neighbourhood play

For many parents, the local neighbourhood has gone from being a benign place of socialisation for their children to a dark and dangerous place, fraught with the evils of strangers, traffic, harsh and unforgiving surfaces, child kidnappers and unfriendly neighbours. Yes, it's true that the proliferation of the motor car has made it difficult to roam about as easily as we did when we were young (unless your kid has got hold of a fake driver's licence), but in truth the threat posed to children in their own streets is grossly exaggerated. Having playmates in the same street is a blessing for you and your child, particularly if they prefer to go and play at the other family's house. Today, play-dates (themselves a modern invention with all the ghastly connotations of diaries, personal assistants and time-poor executives) have to be organised well in advance—where now the spontaneous gathering of kids in the street to steal apples from Mr Williams's orchard or skip pebbles in the stream? Or whatever urban equivalent you can think of other than tagging and dealing in recreational drugs.

COMPETITIVE SPORT

I personally have never been that keen on competitive sport, but I understand that there are those who take an interest in it—apparently, there are television programs and sections of the newspaper devoted to the subject. From what I can gather, competitive sport is an area best left to the professionals; they're qualified, they're trained and happy in the knowledge that they'll lead dull and meaningless lives when their knees give out. But if you insist on introducing your child to their tawdry world, here are a few habits to avoid:

162 Thinking it's you playing the game instead of your child

The unedifying spectacle of parents hollering abuse thinly disguised as encouragement from the sidelines of children's sporting events is becoming increasingly frequent—so much so that sporting bodies have taken steps in an attempt to control it. Soon, under-ten fixtures will have to be held at secret locations in friendly off-shore nations. By all means shout 'Well played!' or 'Not to worry—you'll win next week!' or even at a pinch 'Tackle the fat one—he's slower!', but try to avoid admonishing your child for their lack of sporting prowess in public. Save that for when you get home behind closed doors. Similarly, avoid confrontations with parents from opposing teams on the sports field; it doesn't set a good example to the children. Save that for when you get behind closed doors as well.

163 Thinking you know more than the referee

Look, you may well know more than the referee, but seeing he's usually only twelve years old and doing a favour for his younger sister and her soccer team, there's little point in letting everyone else know how well versed you are in the rule book. Yelling 'You're a fucking idiot, ref—Helen Keller could've seen that that was out!' at someone only just starting high school doesn't reflect well on you. For a start, the ref will probably have never heard of Helen Keller and may in fact confuse her with Amanda Keller, prominent television identity, who is fully sighted, thus rendering your abusive analogy somewhat pointless.

164 Identifying as a soccer mum or dad

A term much favoured by politicians—why don't they ever refer to the 'jazz ballet mums and dads' or the 'chess club mums and dads'? Well, to be fair, I suspect there are few votes in it, particularly in the marginals, but I find the phrase 'soccer mums and dads' patronising and banal. Admittedly, as games

The Active Child

go, soccer is an improvement on full-contact sports, although my own experiences of the beautiful game were desultory affairs and, due to the fact that my foot-eye coordination is of an even lower standard than my hand-eye coordination (even when upside down), after a few games at left full-back I was demoted to linesperson. This called for stamina, judgement and authority, none of them my long suit, and frankly, I couldn't really care less who touched the ball last so my flag-waving was constantly overridden by the referee.

Anyway, junior soccer these days has become an industry, largely fuelled by voluntary slave labour. The season seems to be year-long. Parents spend every waking minute of the weekend ferrying their kids to remote playing fields, drawing up team rosters, group emailing fixture details, coaching, washing the uniforms and abusing the players of opposing teams. Perfectly interesting people turn into complete dullards who can talk of nothing but soccer and the over-thirties team they've joined so they can share their kids' interest. If your child wants to play soccer, let her move to Liverpool or Manchester.

165 Wanting your child to become an Olympic swimmer

Sod that for a game of soldiers—arise every morning at 5 a.m. to watch Junior plough up and down an indoor pool with the smell of chlorine permeating your hair and verruca warts growing in your feet as you sit bored rigid in the steamy damp? No thanks, Doctor. Not to mention all the extra food they'll need. Realistically, what chance have they got of making the Olympic squad? About as much as you have. And even if they should get picked, what chance of a medal? They'll spend four years training for a mere fifty-eight seconds in a first-round heat, managing a plucky seventh place. And you'll have to fly over there to sit up in the stands with your boxing-kangaroo flag, verrucas giving you grief, trying to look enthusiastic. And what are your kids left with at the end of the day? Nothing but disappointment and big shoulders.

166 Encouraging your child to take up an unusual sport like fencing

Ditto curling, croquet, lacrosse, decathlon or extreme macramé. You're only doing it to make yourself look good, wanting Tarquin to be 'different', whereas I'm sure he'd much rather play basketball and eat McDonald's.

167 Getting too much into netball

There's something about netball that I find unattractive. It may stem from the time when our local park was covered in tarmac so netball could be played there twenty-four hours a day—I've been set against the code ever since. I know a lot of people like it—many passionately—but frankly, netball isn't very cool and if you encourage your child to play it, they won't be cool either. It also means that you'll have to stand about with people who aren't cool and sign endless petitions asking TV stations to lift the profile of the sport.

168 Telling your child that winning isn't everything, it's the only thing

It's good for a child to be competitive—a game is only worth playing if it's played to win, but the gracious loser is becoming an endangered species. As, indeed, is the gracious winner. Fist-pumping and grunting might be tolerable at Wimbledon, but they look out of place at a junior holiday tennis camp. Discourage your child from showing outward signs of triumphalism. Tell him that a quiet, laconic nod to the pavilion when he reaches a century is more than enough—we don't really need a victory lap every time he scores a leg bye.

This page can be folded to demonstrate that few paper planes
fly very well.

15

INDOOR FUN!

'It should be noted that children at play are not playing about; their games should be seen as their most serious-minded activity.'
Montaigne

This page is a pre-made origami doormat.

A rainy day doesn't mean any less fun in the household of the ineffective parent—chances are the fun never really took off in the first place. Children get bored easily, but resist the temptation to just sit them down in front of the TV or computer. There are plenty of old-fashioned games that can provide minutes of entertainment for the whole family.

Make Your Own Playdough

So easy and much more affordable than the stuff you buy in the shops! And a great opportunity for the kids to have fun in the kitchen. You'll need:

- 2 cups plain flour
- 4 tablespoons cream of tartar
- 2 tablespoons cooking oil
- 1 cup salt
- 2 cups water
- food colouring

Combine ingredients in a saucepan. Mix on low heat until you realise the recipe said tablespoons, not teaspoons. Discard glutinous mess. Scrub saucepan in futile fashion then also discard. Combine ingredients, realise child has eaten half of the cup of salt; assist with vomiting, clean bathroom. Return to stovetop to retrieve boiled-over contents of saucepan. Cool, turn out onto kitchen benchtop and knead vigorously—encourage the children to join in.

Hose down children in the shower and place semi-liquid playdough mixture in fridge. Retrieve in semi-liquid state two hours later. Turn on TV to distract kids. Place mixture in freezer. Retrieve still mysteriously semi-liquid mixture, discard and go to Woolies to buy commercial playdough. Return to find children have completely lost interest. Make unrecognisable shapes by yourself and ruin everything by mixing colours together.

CUBBYHOUSE FUN

Remember the fun you used to have making cubbyhouses as a kid? The endless hours of playing at secret societies, camping, or cowboys and indigenous Americans? Cubbyhouse building is an activity that requires only hours of cleaning up afterwards.

STEP ONE

Get out every blanket, doona and sheet you possess. Assemble all soft toys in the house and help the kids assign names.

Indoor Fun!

Three hours later, pull the dining room apart to provide the chair framework for your cubbyhouse.

STEP TWO

Arrange chairs in a structural pattern then attempt to attach blankets etc. to same. Try clothes pegs, g-clamps, hair ties, string. All useless. Turn on TV to distract kids. Finally use duct tape to assemble low-profile structure with alarming sag in the roof that can only be held up with a broom and a mop. Discourage cat from collapsing entire edifice by sitting on the roof. Line floor with doona, cushions etc.

STEP THREE

Cautiously enter the cubbyhouse and encourage children to do same by turning off the TV and threatening to remove it from the house entirely. Once children inserted, carefully reverse out and prepare healthy snacks.

STEP FOUR

Deliver afternoon tea to the cubbyhouse—originally planned as lunch, but delays to construction have forced back the schedule. Inadvertently destroy structure and upset snack and drinks trays by clipping the broom as cramp in leg forces rapid return to an upright position. Ruin everything, acknowledge shortcomings as parent and consign doona to dry-cleaning pile that has been steadily growing in laundry. Return everything to linen cupboard, dining room and toy box then retire, shattered, for early night with a bottle of something cold and white.

Board Games

Even in this digital age of computers and iPods, the humble board game can provide a lot of entertainment. Introduce your children to murder with Cluedo, test their ability to draw and complete lack of lateral thinking in a game of Pictionary or highlight the inequities of free-market capitalism with the classic Monopoly.

Here's how a Monopoly afternoon might pan out:

- Set up game. Hunt for missing title deed to Whitechapel and the top hat.
- Assign tokens and argue about who gets the top hat recently retrieved from inside the video player
- Assign banker, bearing in mind how badly your child is doing in maths
- Discuss how stealing money from another player is inappropriate behaviour
- Reassure that second place in beauty contest is not reflection of personal worth
- Settle argument over Park Lane and Mayfair
- Redistribute player's assets after he/she leaves game because dissatisfied with coming last
- Encourage one of the remaining players to regurgitate dice
- Inform group that Brian-in-kindergarten's daddy is in jail for different reasons
- Explain that hotels cannot be constructed without four houses on each property within same group—suggest everyone reads the bloody rules

Indoor Fun!

- Try to explain the concept of a mortgage, even though having trouble grasping it yourself
- Pray for merciful release from interminable game with no clear winner
- Retrieve game pieces from four corners of the room when swept from the board in an imperious gesture of frustration by child now coming last
- Retire hurt amidst general tears and confusion

Let's Make Cookies!

Let's not.

Hide-and-Seek

For some reason, young children are endlessly fascinated by hide-and-seek. No-one knows why. Similarly, no-one knows why they are reluctant to play it without parental involvement. Personally, I can think of better things to do than hole up in a cupboard for half an hour as they ineffectually search the house until I'm forced to emerge from hiding to yell 'Oh for God's sake, I'm in here!' However, if you do feel duty bound to play, here are a few tips to make the whole thing more bearable:

Hide in a neighbour's house. That way you might get a cup of tea and a biscuit

Always elect to be the seeker

Count to a thousand—cuts down the number of times you'll have to play

THE 700 HABITS OF HIGHLY INEFFECTIVE PARENTS

Hide on top of a cupboard—small children rarely look up

Remove power fuse if playing at night—total darkness makes hiding much easier

Remember that children can't stay still for long; sooner or later they will betray themselves

Encourage found child to reveal where siblings are hiding

Schools

As your preschooler approaches her first day at big school, you can demystify the whole process by playing schools at home. Even children attending school full-time like to play schools, especially if they can be the teacher. Unfortunately, if a parent is assigned that role, the students expect lesson plans, sport and endless show-and-tell, where every available toy is dragged out to be introduced to the classroom. Here are a few tips to make the game both fun and educational:

Set challenging maths questions. Every day is a learning day and it helps them to remember that you know more than they do.

Forbid craft that involves glue, glitter or paint. Colouring in is usually painless, especially if you don't make the pencils too sharp.

Teach them things not taught in today's schools—coastal rivers, kings and queens of England, colonial history or (depending on where you live) grammar, spelling, respect, arithmetic, discipline, manners, etc.

Indoor Fun!

Give them a taste of what school was like in your day and watch the surprise on their faces as you bring out the cane!

Encourage them to get out their busy books for free time, giving you the chance to swan off for a bit of pupil-free time in the staff room

Play boarding schools and suggest an early lights out

Cards

Playing cards provide games as old as time itself. The Chinese had cards in the ninth century and 400 years later they reached Europe, which just shows how slowly people travelled back then. Start your kids off with picture cards for a game like Happy Families or any of the contemporary equivalents. The ancient game of Snap, or Wars as it's sometimes known, is always guaranteed to end in a punch-up and frayed nerves of anyone else in the house with the explosive burst of **SNAP!!** every few minutes. As they get older, teach them strategy with games like stud poker and remember that children have excellent memories—train them to memorise the pattern of two packs of dealt cards, then dress them up for a family night at the casino!

Use this page as a shopping list then leave it at home.

16

DINNERTIME!

'"Home-made veal-and-ham-pie! Stuffed tomatoes! And what a salad ... radishes, cucumber, carrot, beetroot, hard-boiled eggs, tomatoes, peas—Joanna, you're a marvel! And lashings of ginger beer—what is the pudding?" George asked.'
Enid Blyton, Five on a Secret Trail

Use this page as a weekly menu planner. As if.

Nice try, Enid. What is the greatest challenge for any parent: preparing a child to live an independent and happy life? Teaching right from wrong? Keeping your child safe and healthy?

None of the above, in fact. It's working out what to feed the buggers—not only during the crucial formative months but three times a day thereafter, every day for the next 6570 days. And that's only if they can cook by the age of nineteen or leave home shortly thereafter, which is a very big if. Forget running a major corporation or being the prime minister; without a doubt, the most challenging job you can tackle in life is running a successful family kitchen.

Anxiety doesn't help. New parents nervously monitor their baby's nutritional intake; some mothers struggle to breastfeed and are crippled by guilt and then have to brave the dreaded transition to solids, losing sleep over vegetables, juvenile diabetes, obesity, allergies, intolerances, sugar levels, additives, junk food, canteen rosters, fluoride, and every perverse rejection of what you know is delicious food by picky eaters. Mealtimes in the early years can become a performance in themselves, parents hovering either side of the highchair coaxing baby to open wide for the choo-choo train, or making teddy bear–shaped broccoli mash-cakes in a vain attempt to get Junior to ingest something green other than playdough.

As your child gets older, boredom becomes your greatest enemy. Preparing school lunches, attacked with such gusto in the early days, begins to resemble *Groundhog Day*, an endless repetition on the basic theme of bread, Vegemite and any other filling not proscribed by the school's allergy list. Pre-packaged snacks, frowned upon by anyone *not* making school lunches, start to furtively find their way into lunch boxes. In a moment of pure frustration, you may be tempted to throw in a peanut-butter sandwich, just so you can see if the teachers' training with the EpiPen is up to it and their peanut-allergy response times meet the national standard.

Children, being notoriously picky eaters, will routinely declare they don't like something even before tasting it. I'm sure if string beans were pink instead of green, small girls would not be so averse to them. But cast your mind back to your own childhood—were you expected to eat Thai food or sushi? Avocados only existed in exotic restaurants as an alternative entree to the prawn cocktail. No child was expected to eat capsicum, and fish had more bones in it than an ossuary (house of bones if you're puzzled by the analogy). This pressing contemporary need for a child to broaden its palate escapes me.

Because the number one habit of ineffective parents in the area of feeding their children would have to be:

169 Forgetting that no small child ever starved itself to death

Cats, notoriously picky eaters, can actually starve themselves to death even when edible food is on offer. To my knowledge, no small child has ever done so. Of course, the situation is entirely different when they're older, but anorexia and other serious eating disorders don't begin until there is a more highly developed sense of self, albeit a distorted one; the great irony of the capacity for rational thought that separates us from other animals is our equally developed propensity to irrational thought. Babies, on the other hand, are designed to eat and, given the opportunity, will happily regulate their own dietary intake. Unless your child is patently failing to thrive, you're probably giving them enough food.

170 Having a nervous breakdown over your inability to breastfeed

Can't say I've ever lost sleep over that one, but this is certainly a hot-button issue in parenting circles. If you're unable to breastfeed, it's often not your buttons that are hot; it's more likely to be your nipples—hot, cracked and red-raw. At a time when women most need understanding and sympathy, the mother who has difficulty breastfeeding is usually met with raised eyebrows, mutterings and condescension. So much for the sisterhood! Obviously, breastfeeding is the best and easiest method of nourishing a baby—it's the way nature designed it. But nature also designed the appendix, bubonic plague and acne, so plainly some things in nature are a work in progress or don't always go according to plan.

The mother unable to breastfeed is faced with a barrage of useful information to make her feel inadequate. Clearly, it's of benefit for public health programs to encourage breastfeeding but perhaps, as the pendulum swings back towards a greater acceptance of the practice (and it's strange to think that it ever went out of fashion), the psychological stick is getting larger than the carrot. Some touted studies of the benefits are of marginal value—one on the effect of breast milk on the incidence of middle-ear disorders in the under-twos ended with the useful advice: 'Limiting early child care in large groups might also be advisable'. Similarly, a study on IQ differences between breast- and bottle-fed babies at age seven concluded that genetic inheritance may play a part.

Luckily, giving your child any breast milk at all is better than giving her none. Even a few weeks will be beneficial; if you can express milk, so much the better. There is no doubt that breastfeeding is the preferred option, but if it can't happen, don't worry. Honestly, even in the developed world, your child faces far greater threats to her health, intellectual development and wellbeing than being raised on bottled formula.

171 Thinking bottle feeding will be easier

Having said all that, there are parents who give away breastfeeding for reasons other than inability. They may be cultural, social or economic; it's hard to breastfeed when you need to return to full-time work. But don't make the mistake of thinking bottles will be easier. As someone who has been down the path of Milton sterilisers, bottle warmers and endless washing up, I can assure you it's not. Our twins were five weeks premature and their sucking reflex had not developed; they were tube-fed with expressed breast milk while in hospital and at home, but eventually it all became too difficult and, after an exhaustive battle, we decided to shift onto formula. Much as I'd like to pin the children's shortcomings on that decision, in all honesty, I can't. And as far as we can tell, formula has had no effect on them other than to reduce their financial inheritance.

There are advantages to bottle feeding. They make it easier for your child to be cared for by someone else. The workload can be shared and fathers have a chance to bond with their small children at mealtimes as well. Before they learn to talk. And talk back.

172 Breastfeeding as a political statement

Look, I think it's absolutely marvellous that you're breastfeeding and go ahead, feel free to give baby a snack wherever and whenever you want. But do please try to avoid the 'Look at me, I'm exercising my right to breastfeed, you patriarchal tyrants' opportunity. I can't really see the need for anyone to sling one out to feed Earth, Charity or whatever herbal name they've conferred on their offspring during, say, a panel discussion program on TV, or while attending question time in the Senate. Precisely who are they doing it for?

173 Breastfeeding for too long

I don't mean in terms of minutes; no, this is the rather more delicate question of how many months or years. It's very much a question of personal taste and needs. My eye was recently drawn to a YouTube clip—during research you understand—about a woman who was still breastfeeding her 8-year-old daughter. Apart from the fact that it looked like a sketch from *Little Britain*, something didn't seem quite right. But who are we to judge? Still, might be better if she can give it away before high school.

174 Delaying the move onto solids

There are certain milestones in a young child's life that are approached with trepidation by the inexperienced parent. Potty training is one; solid food is another. Apart from the spectacular bowel movements that need to be attended to, the transition to solid food is no big deal in retrospect. Indeed, everything about parenting is no big deal in retrospect. It's just a pity we can't retrospect at the time.

Solids are introduced into a child's diet from around six months. Begin with something like pureed fruit, potato or avocado—anything mild and all but tasteless in small portions. This will accustom your child to airline food. Move onto more complex tastes as they get older. Remember: no hard fruits or nuts, because they are a choking hazard, and never leave your child unattended while he or she is eating. Do not introduce honey before twelve months (danger of infant botulism and/or turning into a bee—true). Low-fat dairy products are not suitable for infants under two years of age.

175 Indulging the fussy eater

Refer to the first habit in this section. If your child doesn't like something, try again. Foods can be rejected up to eleven times before a child develops a taste for it. Mind you, you could offer me offal a hundred times and I still wouldn't take to it. But I dare say I'd be the first to say 'More offal!' if I was starving. Children, as in everything else, need to be educated in the delights of cuisine, but don't overdo it. We all acquire different tastes at different times and no two children move towards appreciating the *Good Food Guide* at the same pace. I knew a child who would eat nothing but minced beef and Ribena, right into the teen years. He survived. He was odd, but he survived.

176 Making mealtime show time

The nervous parent, worried that baby is not eating enough, despite the fact that the highchair is almost touching the floor under his weight, will try any number of tricks to encourage him to eat. I suspect that babies enjoy the spectacle of their parents making fools of themselves more than they appreciate the subtleties of 'Open wide for the food truck to reverse in—Beep! Beep! Beep!' The danger in making mealtime an entertainment is that your child will expect it to be so forever. This is not possible, as experience will eventually show you that family mealtimes are anything but entertaining.

177 Allowing sugar to be introduced into the diet

Be wary of well-meaning elderly relatives who say 'One little sweetie won't do them any harm' as they wave a jelly bean in front of your mesmerised infant. It might not choke them, but it will have a devastating effect on your life from that point on. Their first word will be 'confectionery!', repeated like Chinese water torture every time you stray within two hundred metres of a shop.

Sadly, sugar, fat and salt (the three ingredients that, let's face it, give food any decent taste) are not highly recommended for anyone, let alone children. Trying to limit their intake, however, is about as easy as King Canute trying to limit the tide. As soon as a child has any discretionary spending for the canteen or local shops, it's odds-on the money will be spent on sugar, fat or salt rather than half a kilo of healthy grapes. But as a parent you have to be firm. Obesity levels are rising and chubbiness is a habit learned in childhood. Try for a sensible diet and plenty of exercise and then do the same for your kids.

178 Thinking that 'natural' sweets are okay

Sugar is natural—it grows in the ground. Don't kid yourself that 'natural' sweets are in some way better for your child. Sure, they won't have formaldehyde in them (unless they're off-shore manufactured sweets guaranteed Fill of Nature Goodess!).

179 Stressing about vegetables

Vegetables are very good for you, no argument there. Tricky thing is, not many children voluntarily list vegetables as their favourite food. Of course, you're always going to get the painful types at mothers' group who feed their children nothing but celery and carrot with healthy vegetable-based dips, followed by fruit salad and raw bran, but ignore those people. I'm convinced it's all for show and when the kid gets home they chow down on nothing but burgers 'n' Coke.

Don't feel too guilty about your own feeble attempts to instil a love of vegetarianism in your children. As long as you've made an effort to force capsicum down your child's throat at some point in their lives, rest easy. Most kids would rather not eat vegetables—I know a family where tomato sauce is considered a vegetable—but the palate matures with age and one day they may begin to accept that pickle on the quarter pounder with cheese and discover that not all fluids have to be carbonated. If the child is upright, alert and capable of movement, your nutritional efforts are probably adequate for this stage in life.

180 Giving up on vegetables

Yes, it's true that fruit will provide many of the benefits of vegetables in their absence and kids do take more easily to fruit, especially the expensive ones like strawberries, blueberries, or anything else that comes in tiny punnets from distant places. Pears are also popular, being so sweet, and the staple apple remains a lunchbox favourite for throwing in the bin. But don't give up on the vegies, especially the green variety. With perseverance, you can have your child eating at least one green vegetable on a regular basis. Disguise them in soups, purees and casseroles. Smother them in cheese sauce or form them into novelty shapes: Carrot Man, Broccoli Lion, Cauliflower Armadillo etc. Use your imagination and then imagine your children eating them, because that's probably as close as you'll get.

181 Believing that pizza covers the five food groups

I don't know why kids love pizza so much, but there's something about the combination of dough, ham and cheese that proves irresistible, especially when combined with a DVD.

Some children are happy to include certain vegetables—even fruit in the shape of tinned pineapple—but pizza remains a food high in fat and salt and should only be eaten on special occasions. Try to limit pizza night to any day with the letter 'n' in it.

182 Discouraging your children from cooking for themselves

I once read a book that suggested children should be able to cook their own meals before the age of ten. The thought of children being let loose in a kitchen, with its minefield of knives, gas rings, glassware and other sharp pointy things, would send many a parent into a spiral, even without the vision of how much cleaning up there'll be at the end of it all. But try to encourage your children to attempt simple food-preparation tasks. Show them how you prepare meals: consulting the take-away menu, lifting the phone and preparing the correct change for the driver.

There are cookbooks specifically aimed at children with simple, relatively non-dangerous recipes that they can cook under your supervision. Scrambled eggs, pancakes, poached fish, salads and so on are all quite achievable, but don't expect three-cheese soufflés or stuffed zucchini flowers until at least Grade 5.

183 Allowing children to set the pace at mealtimes

Some children are notoriously slow eaters—one of ours can take two hours to eat a Vita-Weat. Mealtimes become protracted affairs, often dragging on into the early hours of the morning like some awful dinner party, only the guests can't do the decent thing and leave because they're your children. Develop a sensible eating tempo from an early stage—if the food isn't eaten by your toddler in twenty minutes, take it away. Let them learn that food won't appear and remain at their will.

184 Eating together as a family

My sister told me that they didn't really enjoy eating together as a family until their youngest child was at least twelve. I now see her point. The family meal is otherwise known as a fast track to divorce. Feed the kids, preferably in a separate building, then spend quality time with your partner over a decent meal that you actually want to eat. You know, food that doesn't come as a nugget, finger or roll-up.

185 Avoiding eating together as a family

But eating together as a family can be a good way to bond, swap concerns and worries, and exchange news and information, even though it may accelerate the collapse of the family unit. Dining together is a great way to civilise your children, to teach them of the joys of food and cooking and to appreciate the generous bounty that the earth can offer. It worked for the Famous Five.

Honestly, unpleasant as it can be, stick with it, but be warned that the family meal progresses through stages as they grow, each difficult in their own way:

The Highchair Years

Very small children don't so much eat food as fling it at themselves with the hope that some will make it into their mouths. It's difficult to eat together in a sane and relaxing way for the first two years of solid food; most of your attention will be taken up by the children's needs and retrieving mashed broccoli that has been hurled in disgust at the cat. I suggest a few stiff drinks before dinner and then a few more during the procedure.

Highchairs can be brought to sit alongside the dining table, or you can try one of those bosun's-chair affairs that clip onto the side of the table and then fall off at an alarming and inappropriate time, usually when custard has just been served. Line the floors with plastic and have a hose on stand-by.

The Toddler Years

Highchairs have one great advantage: restraint. When your child leaves the elevated safety the highchair offers, your greatest challenge will be to keep the kids at the table, especially if the food is not engaging them. Honestly, they're up and down like yoyos; I get reflux just watching them. Try to get your children introduced to cutlery as soon as possible. I'm still cutting up food for our nine-year-olds (admittedly, the steak's a bit tough when I'm on the barbecue), so make sure you teach them how to handle a knife and fork early. Chopsticks can be saved for later on unless your child has a culturally based aptitude for them, i.e. lives in an area with a lot of Asian-style takeaway outlets that their ineffective parents repeatedly access.

Early School Years

Conversation at the dinner table becomes a problem as their language skills develop. One would think this would be a bonus—you know, holding interesting discussions about the world as their insatiable thirst for knowledge grows with every day. Sadly, no. Who did what to whom in the playground, or at the preschool, fills the conversational agenda with mind-numbing frequency and any attempt to steer the discussion to loftier heights is met with sullen disrespect and an immediate return to who is best friends with whom. Of course, you could take the occasional meal in front of the TV, but the golden years of television are distant memories and it defeats the purpose of a family meal if you're all off watching YouTube on separate monitors.

The Later School Years

As they get older, it becomes difficult to fit a family meal into their crowded schedules. Activities, sports and friends keep them out of the house for longer and more irregular periods. You could always cancel all activities and discourage them from making friends; it'll save on petrol and phone bills and allow for more quality time at home. It may also make your children maladjusted and resentful, but don't worry too much about that—at this stage of their lives they don't like you much anyway.

THE UNIVERSITY YEARS

Family mealtimes at this stage are usually passed in silent resentment—minds churning over thoughts like: 'Why are you still here and why can't you cook a meal yourselves every now and then, you leeching bludgers???' Bear in mind, however, that your children will be thinking exactly the same thing about you when you depend on them in your dotage.

186 Introducing your child too early to grown-ups' restaurants

There are some parents who believe their child is entitled to go anywhere—you know the type; they'll be ineffectually trying to quieten a bawling infant during act two of *Cat on a Hot Tin Roof* or loudly explaining the plot of *The Eternal Sunshine of the Spotless Mind* to a three-year-old at a late-night retro screening in the local art-house cinema. They'll also be seen leaving their child to his own devices in the one expensive restaurant you've come to for a civilised night away from the kids. As you pay $40 for a medallion of veal the size of a fifty-cent piece with a reduced jus and baby carrots, this child will be loudly banging the wine bucket next to you as his parents studiously ignore him. Just because they think their progeny is God's gift to the world, I don't know why we should be expected to share their joy.

Perhaps you should take the opportunity to remind them that there are restaurants designed to be family-oriented that don't mind children running about. And I'm not just talking about the McDonald's variety (although their playgrounds can be useful for smaller children—you can leave them locked in there for hours). No, I'm referring to places that are invariably run by long-suffering yet jolly Italians—a sweeping generalisation, I know, but like all such things, one actually based on truth. These establishments are frequented by like-minded souls—the other patrons are there with their children because they know no-one's going to care about ravioli on the floor or Dora the Explorer being drawn on the walls in crayon. Do make an effort to find these places and take your kids there; don't be selfish and take them to places where people are paying decent money for decent food.

187 Not teaching your child how to behave in a restaurant

However, there comes a time when you can raise the dining bar a little. Eventually your child may want something more than spag bol, ice-cream and a pink lemonade. Teach them how to sit still (try teaching them trigonometry at the same time; it's much easier), use a napkin and consult the available beverages as if they're perusing a wine list. 'Hmm ... the '89 pink lemonade—it's cheeky, perhaps a little presumptuous, but it will sit nicely with the spaghettini con ragout and gelato.' Then sit and wince as they bang the ice bucket at the next table.

TABLE 2
Ideal Menu Plan for School-Aged Children

Day of the week	Breakfast	Lunch	Dinner
Monday	Bran flakes Fresh OJ Wholemeal toast	Rice cakes Fruit	Broiled chicken Broccoli Steamed potatoes
Tuesday	Raw muesli Fruit Milk	Goats cheese Frittata	Grilled fish Bok choy Baked yam
Wednesday	Porridge Banana Honey	Yoghurt Fresh fruit	Lean sausage Mash Cannellini beans
Thursday	Raisin toast Fruit compote Milk	Salad sandwich	Spaghetti Napoli
Friday	Scrambled eggs Wholemeal toast	Sushi Pear with quince paste	Char-grilled lamb Pita bread Baba ganoush
Saturday	Crepes Strawberries Cranberry juice	Crusty ham rolls Apples Chocolate (one piece!)	Spinach pie Green salad
Sunday	Brunch at local trattoria	Carrot sticks Cucumber Hummus Lentil dip	Homemade pizza on stone-ground flour base with eggplant, olives and light mozzarella

TABLE 3
Ineffective Menu Plan for School-Aged Children

Day of the week	Breakfast	Lunch	Dinner
Monday	Nutri-Grain	Canteen ($6—no rubbish, promise)	Chicken nuggets Peas (three) Mash
Tuesday	Bread and Nutella	Vegemite sandwich Banana	Fish fingers Peas (why do I bother?) Oven-baked chips
Wednesday	Porridge Brown sugar cream	Vegemite sandwich Same banana	Spag bol Garlic bread
Thursday	Coco Pops	Baker's Delight cheese and bacon roll	Takeaway
Friday	Bacon rolls	Leftover takeaway	Fresh takeaway
Saturday	Cinnamon toast	Pizza subs Apple (pie)	Sausages Mash
Sunday	Brunch at local trattoria (Macca's)	Popcorn Krispy Kremes	Domino's

I've already told you: do not touch this page!

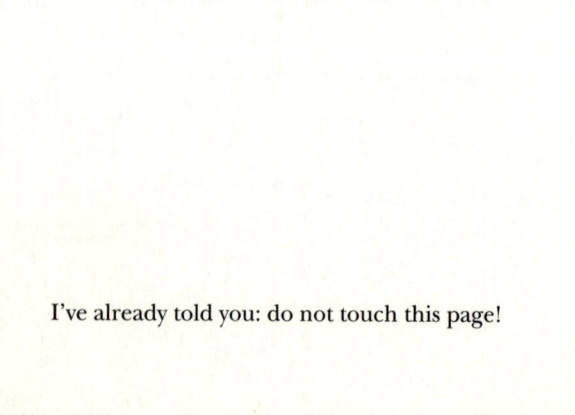

17

THE DISCIPLINED CHILD

'Children today are tyrants. They contradict their parents, gobble their food and tyrannise their teachers.'
Socrates

What did I tell you two pages ago?

What makes a well-mannered child? Every parent dreams of having cheerful, even-tempered offspring who are loving to their extended family, polite to visitors and the people they meet, respectful to their elders and happy to immediately do what they're asked when they're asked to do it by their parents, whom they love and respect with quiet admiration. These children certainly exist in the pages of fiction and, according to our own parents, were as common as cheerful bus conductors and helpful neighbours when they were younger. Where have they all gone?

Indeed, did they ever exist in the first place? Children today are described as being forthright and independent, as having firm opinions, as boisterous, assertive and enquiring. These are seen as good things. Forty years ago we would have called them pushy, strong-willed, arrogant, noisy, obnoxious little shits. Have they changed or is it us?

I really don't know. The modern child, fully aware of his own rights and importance, is determined not only to be seen and heard but also to maintain an inescapable presence in every waking moment. Traditionally, attention seeking was a phase the child grew out of at a relatively young age; now it's all but a profession for anyone under the age of nineteen. Parents seem strangely reluctant to curb their children's behaviour. Admittedly, many of the traditional disciplinary tools have been removed from the parent's behavioural shed, as it were—the swift clip round the earhole; the being sent to a room devoid of computer, TV, stereo and more assorted entertainment than they had on the Tivoli circuit; or even packing the offenders off to some sort of paramilitary outfit like the Scouts or Christian Fellowship.

And please—before you write the indignant letters—I'm not calling for a return to Dickensian values where children cowered in terror of their elders, although a little cowering wouldn't go astray. But the question must be asked: have several decades of this disciplinary reform movement resulted in a more compassionate and outward-looking, less aggressive, nicer generation of human beings? I'm not entirely sure.

188 Being afraid of your own children

I know the feeling—they scare the daylights out of me sometimes too. If your child is an axe murderer, fair enough, but I'm talking about people under the age of ten. The writer Moss Hart said that in dealing with his children he held onto one thought: 'We're bigger than they are and it's our house'. When did we forget this important truth?

The modern parent is not so much afraid of their child as terrified of her reaction. Overly concerned as we are about damaging the child's frail and tender psyche, we are reluctant to mete out any punishment that might meet with his or her disapproval, which somewhat defeats the purpose. In fact, we're reluctant to use the term 'punishment' at all; this is seen as cruel and inhuman treatment that could result in a visit from the Department of Community Services. Instead, we rely on positive reinforcement to discipline our children—the all carrot and no stick approach. All well and good, but when it invariably fails at some crucial point, what can we resort to? The child, ill-prepared for anything vaguely unpleasant, is confused. 'Where is my merit certificate or sticker? A week without television—that is a violation of my human rights! How dare you! I hate you and wish I lived somewhere else.'

Oh no, this trauma could scar her for life—perhaps we should reconsider. 'Alright, two days without television, but one more warning and that's it. Okay, no television for tonight and you can have two more warnings; three strikes and you're out, and this time I mean it, young lady.'

189 Giving in to tantrums

Is there any more destructive weapon in a child's armoury than the tantrum? Best employed in the toddler years, tantrums are originally brought on by the child's frustration, tiredness and obstinacy. Lacking the linguistic skills to negotiate, a two-year-old can't say: 'Look, I appreciate that you don't think it's a good idea for me to put everything on this confectionery shelf into the trolley, but look at it from my perspective—I'm peckish and I think some sort of sugar-based snack would best suit my needs right now'. Instead, they voice their concerns by either screaming, holding their breath, throwing themselves to the floor, head-butting the dairy cabinet, biting your ankles or all of the above. Having gained the attention of everyone else in the supermarket, they continue the performance, pumping up the volume and reinforcing the general perception that you are an awful parent with no control over your child. In your haste to get away from the situation, you reach for the family-sized block of chocolate and thrust it into their hands, making a beeline for the express checkout.

Your child, eventually seeing the success of this ruse, realises he can throw a tantrum at will—there's no need to be genuinely tired and emotional—so he employs it again in the library or at the swimming centre. Having surrendered once, you have no choice but to surrender again.

Here's the hard part: you must never give in to a tantrum, difficult as it is to know how to behave when confronted with your first. Calmly replace the sweets, pick up your child, abandon the trolley and leave the supermarket. Send your partner out to do the shopping when he or she gets back from work—that's why supermarkets have extended hours; they don't want tantrum-throwing children on their premises any more than you do. Comfort your child and try to calm him; any anger on your part won't help the situation because he's confused by the intense depth of emotion he's just felt. He's probably also pissed off that it didn't work.

190 Picking the wrong battles to fight

Children switch off because they get sick of hearing the sound of your voice—unless, of course, you're telling them how marvellous they are; they can't get enough of that. Make sure that you choose the right issues to go on the offensive for—nagging them about a trivial matter just makes it harder

The Disciplined Child

to cut through when something really important comes up. Try grading their misdemeanours on the following scale:

1. Mildly irritating
2. Somewhat annoying
3. Vexing but you can live with it
4. Worth drawing their attention to
5. Deserving of a mild reprimand
6. Needing a raised voice
7. Veiled threat of consequence required
8. Fairly major issue—may need partner drawn in
9. Threatening to the future stability of the family
10. Serious behavioural problem, may need counselling

Take a deep breath and count to ten for anything under a four. Respond calmly to a level-five offence; proceed to code amber for six and seven; red for eight; and ballistic from there on.

191 Not carrying through on a threatened consequence

My favourite is: 'If you don't stop that I'm going to pull the car over and you can walk home'. I must have said that a hundred times and I've only abandoned the children on the side of the road miles from home two or three times at most. Only kidding. It was once and the magistrate told me I can never do it again.

Never threaten any disciplinary measure you're not prepared to carry out. If you're at the zoo, picnic packed and generally ready for a family fun day out after hours of preparation, don't say 'We're going home right now if you don't stop feeding that gorilla' unless you're absolutely prepared to sweep out in a dramatic flurry to get into the car and drive home immediately.

192 Allowing your child to talk back

An offshoot of the 'children have rights' movement, this is also a consequence of the equally modish obsession with respecting a child's opinions, on the assumption that they are rational beings. It is reinforced in the media and entertainment through the emergence of the 'sassy' child: street smart, cynical and always ready with the one-liner comeback. Watch any episode of *Hannah Montana* and you'll see what I mean. Further confusing the boundaries are animated feature films aimed at both adult and child audiences, the idea being that kids like the colour and movement and the long-suffering parents can snigger at the innuendo.

Yes, your child's thoughts and observations are valid and they should be encouraged to voice them, but it's a mistake to think that children can make the sorts of judgements we require for social coexistence: tact, diplomacy, patience, forbearance and an ability to politely overlook the poor behaviour of others. These are skills that we as adults struggle with—why do we expect our children to have acquired them? Nuance is not in a child's vocabulary and until they are mature enough to recognise it, strong and simple rules will save you all a lot of grief. How you enforce them is another matter altogether—if you've got any ideas, let me know.

193 Introducing sarcasm at an early age

I'm not too proud to admit that this was one of my bigger mistakes. They didn't understand it and were confused; by the time they knew what was happening, they were ready to give as good as they got, so now conversation in our house is one cynical drollery after another. I tell you, if I had a life, I'd take it.

194 Not setting boundaries and rules

Contrary to popular belief, children actually like boundaries and routines. Although it's hard to believe, they're often even more confused about how to behave than you are and find the repetition of routines comforting. Likewise, clearly defined rules help them recognise the boundaries of behaviour you expect them to operate within. Just make sure you remember the rules yourself and avoid changing them when memory fails.

195 Setting a rule without informing the other parent

Discipline must be coordinated and consistent—united we stand, divided we fall. The people united can never be defeated, except by other people. Never contradict the behavioural advice of your partner and always let them know when you've made a ruling. Any child worth its salt will play off one parent against the other. (Don't forget: even a child two days old wasn't born yesterday.) Feigning innocence, they'll say 'Mum says it's alright if we watch TV'. Father, unaware that television has just been banned for eternity in another room, will reach for the remote. Enter Mother, outraged, then, as the television is hurled out the window, the children wail, 'But Dad said we could!' Exit Father, speechless, in fit of pique, only to return sheepishly after walking round the block.

196 Believing that a removal of privileges constitutes a punishment

It works in the prison system so why not in the home? A child, subjected to the removal of his Nintendo DS for a few days, will simply revert to his default state of an already privileged existence. If I may draw an analogy from the patisserie, he may temporarily lose the icing but will retain the moist and delicious cake. Hardly devastating. Remove a privilege that means something, like food and water.

197 Being reluctant to echo the words of your own parents

It's a frightening thing when you first hear your parents' words coming out of your own mouth, usually something along the lines of: 'Well, while I'm paying the bills, you'll do what I say' or 'I'm not here just to pick up after you'. For the first few years of your child's life you can restrain yourself but eventually the worm turns. Your initial reaction is to kick yourself for falling into the trap and promise yourself that you'll never say it again. But why worry?

Yes, there are people who have no wish to revisit their childhoods, whose upbringings were less than ideal and who will fight to ensure their own children are not subjected to the same suffering they endured. And rightly so. But I'd hazard a guess that the majority of us have no real complaints about the way we were brought up. Yes, our parents may have made mistakes, but we can be mature enough to realise they were honest ones. Minor grumbles aside, most of us are proud of the job our parents did, or at the very least harbour no long-term resentment and are prepared to settle out of court.

James Dobson, the right-wing nut case who argues that George W Bush was possibly the greatest president in American history, did in fact have something relevant to say when he wrote:

> Sometimes we're so concerned about giving our children what we never had growing up, we neglect to give them what we did have growing up.

He was perhaps, from his own personal perspective, referring to the birch rod, lynch gangs and good ol'-fashun God-fearin', but he has a point. If you can't come up with anything more original and valuable, don't be too quick to ignore the lessons of your own upbringing.

198 Bemoaning the fact that a child needs to be told something ten times

A common complaint—I must have heard it from every parent I know at least ten times. Think about your own behaviour—how many times do you need to be told something before it sticks in your brain? A phone call about an upcoming meeting needs email confirmation, a diary entry, a reminder and a note-to-self and even then you forget it. How can you expect a child to be any quicker on the uptake? These are people who have trouble tying up their own shoelaces.

There are two ways you can tackle this problem in the family. First, have the children's hearing checked. Next, phrase your requests as a positive action, so rather than asking the question: 'Could you get dressed now, please?', say in a brisk and affirmative manner: 'Come on, getting dressed!' And then repeat it ten times.

Alternatively, vary the way you ask them to do something. Suggest a competition—'I bet I can get dressed faster than you can!' Of course, you may already be dressed and will have to undress first, but honestly, you could try on your entire wardrobe in the time it will take them to get it together.

199 Not introducing your child to chores

Grandad used to say: 'Every morning I'd do the chickens, chop the wood and clean out the fireplaces before school. I'd walk three miles there and four miles back, then do the afternoon milking, muck out the pigs and wash the dishes after dinner'. I don't quite know why he said that—he lived in town and wouldn't know what to do with a pig if he fell over it—but dementia has its own funny ways.

Still, it does go to show how different things are these days. The modern child has at its disposal numerous labour-saving devices, otherwise known as parents. When faced with the choice of picking up their dirty clothes yourself or calmly asking the child to do it five times before resorting to shouting and threats of dire consequences, too often you take the easy way out and do it for them. Because it's quicker, less stressful and anything for a quiet life.

But children should be taught household responsibilities, even if you yourself have never moved beyond the domestic standards of the shared house of your youth, where any request for you to tidy up was met with the stock response: 'Hey, if you want to obsess about it, you do it. I'm happy to

The Disciplined Child

live in the mess'. Two hours later you went to pick up your washing, dried and ironed, from your mother.

It takes a lot of effort to instil a work ethic in children, because you will find them strangely reluctant to lift a finger. Start small—laying the table, for example—then move on to something more challenging, like picking up a wet towel (this defeats many adults).

Draw up a useful chart listing the daily chores to encourage your little helpers. If all the squares are ticked by week's end, perhaps you could give a reward like extra pocket money. (I prefer not to call this bribery—think of it as a creative incentive.)

Simply laminate the chart for easy write-on/wipe-off efficiency and stick it on the fridge with all the other crap-on-magnets. Use in a half-hearted way for a few weeks then give it up as hopeless and discard.

Use this page to draw up a birthday party invitation list.

18
IT'S YOUR BIRTHDAY

'"It's bad enough," said Eeyore, almost breaking down, "being miserable myself, what with no presents and no cake and no candles, and no proper notice taken of me at all, but if everybody else is going to be miserable too—"'
AA Milne, Winnie-the-Pooh

Use this page to draw up birthday party invitation list (Part II).

Look in the back section of any of the numerous parenting newspapers and journals that have sprouted like toadstools in the past fifteen years and you'll find page upon page of advertising for children's birthday party services. It's big business for a growing number of clowns, magicians, caterers, petting zoo owners, amusement ride operators, fairies and party shops. Forget one plate of fairy bread and the GI-lime cordial after a few rounds of pass-the-parcel; the modern children's birthday party requires creativity, planning and a big budget, none of which come easily to the ineffective parent.

200 Suggesting a themed birthday party

That's your first mistake right there. You might think you're encouraging creativity, individuality and imagination, but you're laying yourself wide open to a marketing exercise beyond your reckoning and a date with the icing bag in the small hours of the morning as you struggle to meet the novelty-cake deadline. Aladdin, Big Ted, Little Mermaid, Star

Wars, Disney Princess, Bob the Builder, Toy Story, Sponge Bob Square Pants, Teletubbies, Bindi the Jungle Girl, Judy Garland: the Madison Square Garden Days—the list of possibilities is endless for a child's party. But you have to go out and buy the themed stationery, gifts, invitations, cakes and balloons then have the parents of the guests badgering you about costumes.

Or you can say no to the machine and do it yourself. Hand-sketch some characters or photocopy the DVD cover to make invitations; use the dress-up box to put together some outfits that in a bad light look almost nearly like the original and make a cake in the shape of the party's hero. This will take several days and look ordinary. Your child will resent you and spend the afternoon in sullen silence, grabbing presents from his guests and making you look bad just because you wouldn't buy the real Harry Potter invitations and deliver them by owl.

Here's a suggestion for an easy-to-do theme: 'You're six. Get over it'.

201 Holding the party in a fast food restaurant

It's tempting because you know they'll clean up the mess, the children will probably eat the food and best of all it requires no effort on your part beyond booking the place. And fast food, although they shouldn't eat it regularly, is not going to kill them once a year. But how can you surrender to the blatant cultural imperialism of the foreign-owned chain store? Quite easily if they throw in the party bags as well.

202 Holding the party in an indoor play or sports centre

Weatherproof, certainly, and useful if you want to cater for a novelty theme like gymnastics, but ultimately there's something depressing about a kids' party next to a bunch of sweaty blokes playing indoor cricket or beefy girls thundering about on the netball court. Play centres can be equally disheartening because it's rare that you can book the entire place, so you have to share it with screaming toddlers and tired parents at the plastic cafe tables drinking cappuccinos. And who knows what fetid bacteria lurks in the pit filled with coloured balls.

203 Hiring bouncy castles

Bowing to infantile pressure, some parents resort to hiring amusement-park equipment—bouncy castles, merry-go-rounds, inflatable slides or pony rides. Not only do they cost a bomb, someone always gets hurt. It's either an elbow in the eye, being stood on by a disgruntled Shetland, or a child having an unexpected bout of equinophobia, which, the nice doctor at casualty informed me, is an exaggerated fear of horses. The amusement operators always want to get home as soon as possible (well, can you blame them?) and someone bursts into tears because they had one less go than someone else. A cheaper alternative is to have the party in your local park and use the pre-existing equipment. Decorate it colourfully to briefly confuse the guests into thinking it's in some way special.

204 Hiring entertainers on a least-cost basis

A magician or party clown with the appropriate police clearances can make a kids' party zing, but be wary of the less qualified 'entertainers' who have muscled in on this lucrative trade. A pair of wings and glitter cheeks do not necessarily make you an enchanting fairy—in fact, be wary of fairies full stop. There are an awful lot of unemployed arts students out there who will turn up with a jar of pixie dust and some toxic face paints that leave your child's cheeks permanently marked with the outline of a badly drawn butterfly.

Clowns are asking for trouble, as one in five small children suffers from coulrophobia, which, as the nice nurse at the 24-hour medical centre informed me, is an exaggerated fear of clowns. (I have an exaggerated fear that the clown won't be remotely funny, but that's another thing altogether.) And if an entertainer's repertoire of balloon animals only extends to 'snake' and 'spineless puffer fish', chances are she can't hold fifteen six-year-olds spellbound for half an hour.

Under no circumstances attempt to entertain the children yourself once they've passed the age of five. Up until then, children think you're hilarious and enjoy watching you humiliate yourself; after they've hit school, you're little more than an embarrassment.

205 Making a novelty cake

The worst thing you can do is buy a book of character birthday cake suggestions and try to make one yourself. Much easier to head down to the Cheesecake Shop and grab an off-the-shelf Black Forest cake that has about as much Bavarian flavour as you do. However, if you do insist on making a cake from scratch, don't let your kids pick which one they want because they will invariably select the one with an Icing Difficulty of 10 and a decorative scheme that would defeat Michelangelo. Have you ever tried to cut sponge cake into the shape of an octopus? And trust me, two Swiss rolls and a lamington covered with blue icing and lined with chocolate freckles along each side does not look like Thomas the Tank Engine. Even a three-year-old will be disappointed.

206 Expecting your child to appreciate the effort you've made

Why should this day of the year be any different? More often than not, the birthday boy or girl, overwhelmed by all the attention, will have a complete meltdown at some stage of proceedings and throw a spectacular tantrum. This is often at the gift-opening phase or during games, which casts your child in the spotlight as being spoilt, indulged and ungrateful. You know that to be largely true, but you don't necessarily want to share it with everyone else.

207 Expecting the guests to all enjoy themselves

If it's not your child throwing a tantrum, someone else will. Or choke on a jelly bean, or have an anaphylactic reaction to the Buzz Lightyear bars that were guaranteed nut-free. What is it with Chinese manufacturing at the moment? Kids' parties seem to bring out the worst in children—over-hyped by the occasion and the red drink you foolishly served as part of the fire-engine theme, they can behave badly and do things they and their parents will later regret. Not unlike adult parties, really.

208 Buying a piñata

The practice of blindfolded supplicants beating a suspended pot or basket to cause it to spill forth its store of tiny treasures and treats is believed to have originated in China and progressed through medieval Europe to South America through the conquistadors, although evidence suggests the Mayans already had a similar ceremony of pagan significance. How it became de rigueur at birthday parties for six-year-olds in Australia remains a mystery. Combining greed and violence, the piñata seems a perfect party accessory, but in truth they invariably disappoint, either falling apart on the first whack to shower their feeble collection of cheap sweets and plastic novelty junk down upon the line of children yet to have a turn, or resisting all attempts at breaking until they have to be repeatedly run over by a car to placate the line of weeping, exhausted kiddies who wanted to go home hours ago.

Don't attempt to make one yourself by stuffing lollies into a balloon, inflating and then plastering with papier-mâché. This will burst like a gun going off and expel sweets like shrapnel, possibly taking out several eyes.

209 Serving healthy food

The traditional party fare of chips, frankfurters, party pies and sausage rolls, popcorn, Cheezels etc. is now frowned upon—honestly, some of the looks you get, you'd think you were serving up the cordial at Jonestown. It's been given a name by the PC self-appointed authorities who have weaselled their way onto canteen committees: 'sometimes' or 'celebration' food. But even that, apparently, can seriously endanger our children's health and condemn them to a lifetime of diabetes and heart disease. Healthy foods like carrot sticks, hummus, cherry tomatoes and fruit must now be encouraged. For God's sake, it's a party! If you want to throw away the untouched carrot sticks, hummus, cherry tomatoes and fruit after you've handed out the take-home bags of bran bites and dried pear, go ahead. But a child has to learn somewhere that you haven't really partied unless you feel nauseous and light-headed.

210 No alcohol for the grown-ups

In conjunction with unhealthy food, champagne for the adult guests is frowned upon in some quarters as setting a bad example. If it's a decent drop, what's the problem? A cold refreshment is often the only thing that makes these occasions bearable, especially when one enters the party zone, that curious band of three or four months when the parties stack up on every weekend and your children have a far more extensive social life than you ever had. No, I see no problem putting BYO on the invitation—only trouble is, the parents expect you to provide.

211 Preparing elaborate party bags

Children now come home from someone else's birthday party with more gifts than they brought. The party bag has gone from being a few sweets, a temporary tattoo and a musk stick to something that puts an Oscar gift bag to shame. Today's party bag must include at least ten items from the following list:

- Stickers—preferably holographic or enamelled
- Party popper
- Willy Wonka sours
- Laser spinning top
- Colouring pencils
- Activity sheet

- Comic
- *Girlfriend* magazine
- *Boyfriend* magazine (Judy Garland–themed parties only)
- Fruit bar
- Plastic toy
- Smiggle stationery
- Natural confectionery
- Non-allergenic soap
- Discount vouchers for family activities
- Small picture book
- *Star Wars* figurine
- Playing cards
- Disney-character key ring
- Notebook
- Eraser
- Fart putty or novelty whoopee cushion
- Slime
- Pack of M&Ms, Skittles or Smarties
- Lip gloss

From personal experience, the sweets will be eaten to the regurgitation level and the rest of the stuff binned, or put into a box of similarly acquired junk that accumulates in the house like lint in a clothes dryer.

212 Playing non-competitive games

What is the point of playing pass-the-parcel if everyone gets a prize? Surely it would be quicker to by-pass the paper and sitting-in-circle phase of the game and simply distribute the sticker sheets at once. Another misguided attempt by the politically correct to avoid any child feeling disappointed, non-competitive party games include pin the tail on the genetically modified donkey (tail on any part of the body is a winner); musical chairs (chairs are not removed); musical statues (prizes awarded for starting); and partially sighted man's buff.

213 Playing competitive games

Equally pointless because the tears and recriminations ruin an otherwise awful afternoon. If the birthday boy doesn't win, he sulks; if he does, everyone else thinks it's rigged.

214 Arriving with either excessive or inadequate gifts

Gift-giving is a delicate balance between too much and too little. Too much spent on the average gift and you'll be bankrupt within two years of them starting school. Fair dinkum, Grace Jones doesn't go to as many parties as the average 8-year-old girl. Plus, no other parent will thank you if you set the gift bar too high. Don't turn up at a day-care centre acquaintance's party with a pedal car. On the other hand, don't turn up with something you bought at the BP service station on the way. What's a five-year-old going to do with two litres of coolant?

Think about the gifts you're giving. First question to ask: would I like this coming into my house? Combination siren/rattle/alarm noise-making toy—possibly not. Pet shop toy comprising 385 small plastic pieces, each individually designed to avoid detection on the average carpet—possibly not. Movie voucher—yes, please! Make sure you label your gifts, or write what was given in your card. No point in going to all that effort and expense if it's mistaken for someone else's coolant.

215 Opening the gifts then and there

Ignore the eager mother who says 'Oh go on, open ours—we want to see the look on her face'. Anyone who has sat through the orgy of gift-opening that is a child's Christmas knows only too well that this is an activity best done out of sight. Quickly descending into an ungracious and unpleasant display of avarice if attempted during the party, gift-opening is much better left for a calm, reflective time when you can pass judgement and price the gifts in private.

19

THE LEARNING CHILD

'The only people who seem to have nothing to do with the
education of the children are the parents.'
GK Chesterton

This page can be used for birthday party invitation list (Part III) or dregs unlikely to make the final cut.

One of the more depressing things I've seen lately was a day-care centre advertising: 'Give your child the competitive edge with our fully integrated computer room'. What? Why would anyone want to give a toddler a competitive edge, let alone introduce her to Excel spreadsheets? What's wrong with playing in the sandpit and eating paint?

Sadly, education is now a race to see who can get to the top of the class, into the selective school or the better university place. For many parents, the race cannot begin soon enough. Prenatal Esperanto classes, flash cards in the nursery, the table of periodic elements mobile dangling above the change table. Tutors at the age of five, homework in kindergarten and a pressing campaign for school league tables and class rankings to be made public. If the child's as thick as custard and you've got plenty of disposable income, buy a place at an expensive private school. Or if you're afraid of other people's religious beliefs, cloister them away in a faith-based school that preaches brotherly love in a ghetto. The concept of free universal education that certainly didn't do us any harm is being eaten away and I believe it's up to us as parents to reinstate the values and principals that served us all so well.

Education is not a sprint won by the fastest and best trained. It's a lifetime fun run that will sometimes canter along, often meander and even come to a dead halt now and then as you decide you'd rather watch daytime television for a month than use your brain. But it keeps going. The most important thing you can instil in your child is curiosity and a love of learning; if you can do that, they'll do the rest.

216 Wanting your childcare centre to be fitted with a 'fully integrated computer room'

Don't be so bloody ridiculous. It's a playground, not a business institute. Yes, your child will learn at a childcare centre—he will learn about other children, carers, routines, textures, shapes, colours, food, nap-time, craft, letters, books, pictures and a whole heap of other things, but the last thing he needs is to sit like an automaton in front of a computer. Children have already been sentenced in absentia to a lifetime of that; let them have some freedom for a few years at least.

217 Worrying about where your child will go to school

One of the great dilemmas of our time is the paralysing multiplicity of choice. We now have to choose so many things: mobile-phone plans, super funds, power suppliers, governments, religions or the best cable-TV subscription that adequately caters for our love of sport, lifestyle channels *and* world movies. Unfortunately, education is now no different. There was a time when your kid went to the local schools. Now they can go anywhere. Sensitive child with an interest in music theatre? No problem, send them off to Montessori and then the performing arts school. Sporty type with little interest in academia? Off they jog to the school with a good football program. Dullard with little aptitude for self-motivated learning? Surely there's a private school willing to take them off your hands if the price is right.

My advice is forget about all that and send your kids to the local school, just like in the old days. It's cheap, convenient and part of the local community. Best of all, you don't have to drive them anywhere.

218 Forgetting that children learn in many different ways

Children often learn the most when you don't think they're learning at all—they absorb so much through mere contact with the world, through observation, exploration and experiment. We often overlook the vital importance of play and downgrade its value, particularly in the early school years when, moving into a formalised educational setting, we want our children to 'learn' more in the classroom and spend less time doing seemingly frivolous things. We forget that the best way to prepare a child to read is to read to her; simply by sitting beside you and looking at the picture book as you read the text, hearing the sentence structures and the context, and watching the shapes of the words, a child can set the foundations for literacy. The principles of arithmetic can be learned at play; rudimentary biology can be grasped by exploring the garden and basic aeronautic principles painfully explored by jumping off the garage roof with a cape. (First Aeronautic Principle: capes are all but useless in a flight situation.)

219 Forgetting that you are your child's greatest teacher

Aside from the lessons of Life, there's a lot for you to do. What do you know about calculus? Better start boning up on all that stuff you learned at school that you've completely forgotten! Here's a simple equation without any of that tedious algebra to remember:

School is less than or equal to half the total sum of what your child will learn.

220 Devolving your child's education to others

Devolve *verb (trans)*: to transfer or delegate powers to a lesser authority. Especially relevant if you choose to send your kids to a private school. Don't assume that just because you've paid for it your responsibility ends there or that teachers should do it all (see equation above).

221 Not allowing the teachers to teach

Having said that, don't make the mistake of thinking that you know more about education than educators. There is nothing worse than the parent who hovers over a teacher's shoulder unwilling to let them do their job. They are trained for the task; follow their advice and support them. You don't advise the dentist on how best to fill your child's teeth—unless of course you are a dentist yourself. If I could extend the metaphor, your job in the surgery is to listen, observe and reinforce the lessons learned in the chair: adequate brushing, dental hygiene, flossing and a sensible diet.

Funnily enough, education is a lot like dentistry—you don't always want to attend, it's expensive and sometimes uncomfortable, and the results aren't always immediately obvious, but life without it is miserable and unfulfilled and leaves a bitter taste in the mouth.

222 Expecting a computer to teach your child

I'm yet to be convinced of the value of computers in early education. (Not that I'm a trained educator, but since when has not being qualified stopped anyone having an opinion?) Don't think for a minute that children need to be trained how to use them—within minutes, a six-year-old will know more about computers than you do.

But there's an old saying in teaching that the secret lies in 'talk and chalk'. I believe that's particularly true in the early years and a reliance on technology denies the vital human engagement that children need in order to learn. Yes, computers do offer some educational programs, particularly in maths and literacy, that can benefit your child, but they do little to develop a child's memory, lateral thinking and intellectual creativity. Later in life, they can be useful, but in the formative years they become yet another service provider that do for a child what she should be doing for herself.

223 Accelerating your child's learning

We know that most parents, despite all evidence to the contrary, regard their children as gifted and talented in some way and we've all met parents who want to accelerate their child through the education system. Usually the budding genius is described as being bored, facing no challenges, way ahead of his classmates and in desperate need of stimulation. To you he's a normal, disruptive pest with the attention span of a grapefruit but to Mater and Pater he's the next Stephen

Hawking, although hopefully without the degenerative disease. The inevitable career trajectory for these children is to be moved into a class where they struggle to keep up with the truly exceptional and end up resentful and disillusioned with learning.

On the other hand, there are a few kids who are genuinely super bright and may benefit from a bit of a push. But ask yourself this: what are you accelerating them to? What benefits of a normal school life are they missing out on by being sent to an opportunity class? If I may draw an analogy from the open road: the car that accelerates the fastest runs out of petrol first. Use that as you will.

224 Insisting that your child be given homework

There is an alarming trend for children as young as kindergarten age to be given homework. Most of the teachers I've spoken to tell me that it's at the parents' insistence, in the misguided belief that more work means better work. To my mind, this is completely counterproductive in the short term and possibly damaging in the long. After six hours at school the last thing a tired child needs is homework. For the first few years, it's going to be a test of the parent more than anything else because they're usually the ones who end up doing it, having given up the fight to drag their recalcitrant children to the study table. This is particularly true of projects for Science Week—there's no way a seven-year-old built that working model of Yellowstone Park or has the slightest understanding of a spectrographic analysis of a rainbow.

225 Forgetting that you and your kids help make a great school

A school is much more than the teachers and facilities—an active and engaged student and parent body makes all the difference. A school works best when it reflects and understands the community it serves—you're part of the community so become part of the school. And yes, you have to go to the parent-teacher meetings and volunteer for the fundraising committee. If you're afraid of crowds, don't panic—you'll always meet the same five people.

226 Changing schools at the first sign of a problem

I hated the first four years of high school. I was sent to an all-boys school that specialised in maths, science and sport—hardly a nurturing environment for a delicate hothouse flower of my artistic sensibilities! My parents ignored my pleadings to be transferred (although quite where I would've gone escapes me) and in retrospect, it was the best thing they could've done. I was given a solid education, met an inspirational English teacher in the senior years and fled my alma mater with an inbuilt ability to kick against a system that didn't much care for what I wanted to do.

Sadly, the system—and many other systems just like it—are still indifferent to my endeavours, but the point remains: don't move your child from a school just because they don't like it. You're not meant to like school *all* the time. There is drudgery in everything and life is not fair—these are all valuable lessons for a child to learn and he's not going to learn them if he's wrapped in cotton wool and asked to go (sent is, like, such a negative word) to a school that needs a parental permission slip before it can offer any constructive criticism of his portfolio.

Obviously, if your child is being held upside down in a toilet bowl while the soles of his feet are beaten with a cricket bat, it might be an idea to think about alternatives.

227 Confusing children's inherent behaviour with bullying

When does a kid's natural tendency to teasing and petty meanness become bullying? And let's not pretend that your child doesn't do it: they *all* do it to some degree, even the nicest ones. But it's largely harmless, part of the jockeying for social position that occurs in the playground just as it does in the outside world, and your child's ability to deal with it is integral to his or her future happiness.

Children, particularly girls, can be unbelievably cruel. Having two older sisters, I know. School becomes an endless shifting of loyalties, allies and enemies, and each child gets a turn at being on the receiving end of the group's animosity. You can't stop it—your job is to give your child the resilience to earn the self-esteem to rise above it, and to instil in her a sense of justice and compassion that will show her the futility of such behaviour as she matures. Good luck!

It's when the tide doesn't turn or the focus doesn't shift to someone else that it becomes bullying. Sometimes it's simply not enough to expect a child to stand up for himself. Systemic bullying is a problem best dealt with by experts; it's an issue that has been the subject of much research and there are some encouraging developments in how to deal with it, especially in the areas of restorative justice and mediation. If you think your child is being genuinely bullied, alert their teacher and make sure the issue is followed up. But first make sure you're **not** crying wolf.

228 Refusing to recognise the bully in your own child

An awkward situation—much as we whinge about our children's behaviour, it's very difficult for us to acknowledge behaviour that is genuinely unacceptable and take the steps to remedy it. At the same time, we have to trust our children and not leap to the conclusion that they are to blame for everything. Bullies are usually motivated by issues in their own lives unrelated to the victims they persecute—if you suspect your child is a bully, there may be some painful soul-searching that you'll need to do yourself before you can help your child. Unfortunately, it's often a parent's inability to do that which causes the problem in the first place.

ROLE MODELS FOR THE INEFFECTIVE PARENT

Number Three

THE OLD WOMAN WHO LIVED IN A SHOE
(AND OTHER FAIRYTALE PRIMARY CAREGIVERS)

> There was an old woman who lived in a shoe
> She had so many children she didn't know what to do
> She gave them some broth without any bread
> Then whipped them all soundly and put them to bed

Yes, like to see her try that now. Department of Community Services would be there before the neighbours in the Shoe across the road could call *Today Tonight*.

Mother Goose, the Brothers Grimm, Hans Christian Andersen—the stories we all read to our impressionable children, mouths agog as they sit there entranced, or more probably wondering what's on the Disney Channel. Have you ever actually listened to these stories? Is this really the sort of thing we want our children to be hearing: tales of cannibalistic wolves, dead pigs, duplicitous cats wearing boots, and child molesters? Even worse, take a look at the portrayals of the parents. All either impoverished, mean spirited, incompetent, at death's door or clean through the other side.

Exhibit A: the Old Woman Who Lived in a Shoe. First thing you notice—apart from the shoe/accommodation business—is that there's no sign of the Old Man. Not altogether surprising: your average Old Man wouldn't hang round a shoe for long; no, he'd be off looking for a nice bird with her own boot. And, preferably, no bloody kids! So we immediately realise it's a salutary tale against the perils of having too many children, with the deeper underlying message that life was a lot better before they all came along. Fair enough, we've all felt that at one time or other if we're perfectly honest.

Secondly: the Old Woman 'didn't know what to do'. Incompetent or at her wits' end, either way it's not a pretty picture and she's probably had one or two more chardonnays than she should have while she was cooking dinner, if you could call it that. 'Broth'—hardly a balanced meal! Where are the green vegetables, or at the very least frozen corn? 'Without any bread' ... seems like she didn't get to Baker's Delight and had no back-up loaf in the freezer. Hopeless. 'Whipped them all soundly' ... look, tempting as that might be, it doesn't do a great deal of good in the long run. Having said that, I was no stranger to the odd firm clip around the ear as a child and it didn't do me any harm, although sometimes I have trouble recongsiing wrod shaeps.

Elsewhere in the fairytale and nursery-rhyme genre, the parents are even worse. Jack's mother—if you're going to send your child to market with a cow (which by the way is the only thing you own) you have to set some boundaries. Did she specifically say, 'Do not buy magic beans'? Had Jack been taught about stranger danger at the local village school? Apparently not. And what were the parent body of Hamelin thinking? Likewise Hansel and Gretel's caregivers. If you can't make a go of woodcutting, reskill and find suitable employment elsewhere. Don't abandon your children in the woods, particularly in a district zoned for gingerbread houses.

But the real villains of the piece are those who enter the family through a second marriage: the wicked stepmothers. They were more common in years gone by, despite what one might assume given contemporary divorce rates. In those days, many women died in childbirth and it was common for the father to remarry as quickly as possible. Why they invariably chose wicked women bent on making their stepchildren's lives a misery remains a mystery.

Exhibit B: Cinderella's vacuous father and evil stepmother. Obviously, in mourning and mindful of his daughter's needs, Mr Cinderella married unwisely on the rebound. The ugly sisters should have given him some sort of hint that things were not going to go smoothly, but why, like so many other father figures in the canon, was he such an ineffectual walk-over? The Brady Bunch only made a go of it because they worked at it—endless mediation in the den, Alice's wise words soothing sibling rivalries, Mike and Carol trying any tack they could to make the kids live together in perfect harmony, just like ebony and ivory on my piano keyboard etc.

And Evil Stepmother clearly knew nothing about the teen years. Cinders was at that awkward age—of course she was going to go to the ball, even if she was grounded, with practically no self-esteem after all those demeaning, repetitive chores. Structure household work creatively for children; give them a sense of ownership! It worked wonders for Mary Poppins.

Role Models for the Ineffective Parent

Ironically, fairytales in their original form were intended for adults and children alike. They began life as cautionary tales about unspecified dangers, or allegorical morality stories—the wolf wanting to eat up Red Riding Hood is an allusion to the sexual act and loss of innocence, although he also ate up Grandmother, so he obviously wasn't too picky. Probably would've gone the woodcutter as well if he'd had a chance. *Hansel and Gretel* is a reflection on the realities of the destructive effects of famine. Children in fairytales are exhorted to be brave, independent and clever because in the real world, disease, hunger or violence could carry off their parents at any moment.

Obviously, with improved medical standards and a wide range of takeaway-food outlets, a parent's death from starvation or illness is less likely today in the Western world. Wolves don't pose quite such a threat in, say, Brisbane. If anything, children are more likely to stay at home for much longer, evil stepmothers notwithstanding. So what can we learn from fairytales? Well, if the kids are still living at home in their thirties, drive them to the woods, make sure they've got no pebbles or breadcrumbs, and leave them there.

This page, being near the end of the book, can be safely used as a drinks' coaster.

20

LEFTOVERS: A RANDOM SELECTION OF INEFFECTIVE HABITS

'You will find that as a rule children are a bitter disappointment—their greatest object being to do precisely what their parents do not wish and have anxiously tried to prevent.'
Queen Victoria (in a letter), 1876

Use this page to jot down your own ineffective habits. Use additional paper if required.

229 Giving your child a mobile phone

Having grown up in an age where two cans and a piece of string were regarded by kids as a miracle of telecommunications, it's difficult to accept the amount of money and time that is expended on mobile phones today. Why we are exhorted to keep in constant communication with each other escapes me. Mobile phones erode our memories and steal away the precious joy of solitude. Even a child needs that. There is no reason for any child under the age of fourteen to have a mobile phone, except to pour rivers of money into the pockets of telcos and for texting unreasonable demands to be picked up after soccer.

230 Giving your child free access to computers

Apart from all the nasty types who lurk in the digital shadows of the internet, there's a danger in giving a child too much time 'interfacing' (I believe that's the 'digital' term) with any form of technology. Modern technology, despite the gushing claims of its manufacturers, is essentially dehumanising;

children need to first get a grasp of what the quality of being human actually is before they glibly surrender it to machines. Find some real friends before the virtual besties of Facebook. Learn to put a sentence—or, heaven forbid, a paragraph—together before dumbing down to Twitter. Lurn 2 Spl b4 u txt.

231 Believing that your in-car games will keep the children amused

The modern child is expected to travel more widely than Columbus. Not only do you clock up the kilometres driving to endless weekend engagements, they expect motorhome holidays exploring the great outdoors and New Zealand, air travel to interstate capitals, Disneyland in both Florida *and* California, with a side trip to Euro-Disney and possibly Legoland. In their dreams. But this is a mobile generation.

Very few children enjoy car trips and I've discovered the hard way that even fewer take any pleasure in scenery. CDs and talking books can make a long car trip more bearable, but don't make the mistake of thinking you can press on for another hour before you stop. Ideally, you should stop every fifteen minutes so they can spend an hour playing on the monkey bars. Personally, the appeal of climbing apparatus pales very quickly for me, but hanging upside down on a steel frame is more fun than spending any time in a car with whingeing children.

If you do resort to in-car games, make them challenging. First-to-spot-a-red-car is over in minutes, so get them to hunt down more obscure models—'First to spot an '06 Hyundai Getz with roof rack and spoiler gets an ice-cream'. Resist the temptation to install an in-vehicle DVD player. If you wanted them to sit slack-jawed in front of *Finding Nemo* you could've stayed at home.

232 Planning holidays

Nothing but an open invitation for a child to get sick and the forced cancellation of your plans. In the early years, you won't believe how often this happens. Plan any holiday to take place near adequate medical facilities or invite your GP to come along for the trip as well. Stockpile prescriptions to use at a later date—any sort of antibiotic will do if you've got seats booked and no travel insurance.

233 Choosing your children's friends

Occasionally your child may befriend someone you'd rather wish they didn't. They've probably done it because they're tired of having to make friends with the kids *you* want them to play with. It's another of the myriad subtle ways we shape our children in our own image, which (if God and the creation he fashioned in his own image is anything to go by) is not such a good idea. By all means point them in the right direction.

234 Not giving your children pets

Pets are a great way for your children to learn about the natural world and creatures with which we share the planet—well, at least the ones who won't eat us and we're not particularly eager to eat ourselves. Owning a dog, cat or ferret can teach children how to feed, train and look out for something other than themselves. Pets provide companionship, love and in some cases an exercise outlet to get the kids off the couch, although in my experience cats are reluctant to go for a walk. And I can't see much point in keeping a stick insect.

235 Giving your children pets

Who are we kidding? You'll be the one feeding, walking and cleaning up after any animal you bring into the house. Pets are nothing but an endless drain on the wallet and just tie you down; your children are perfectly qualified to do that, so why introduce competition? Kids don't understand that the cute little puppy is going to grow into a large, fur-shedding, slobbering excrement machine within months. Don't fall for any of that 'He's a stray, he followed us home' crap either. The dog was probably stolen and you'll find his collar stashed under the couch when you next clean there, by which time the dog will be fifteen years old, moulting and dragging its backside all over the polished floorboards.

236 Forgetting the other person in the family—your partner

The arrival of children can have a deleterious effect on any relationship. Their demands make it all too easy to forget that you need to spend time together as an adult couple. You need to talk to each other about something other than the children. Make time for each other; organise 'dates' where you can get out of the house and rekindle the attraction that brought you together in the first place. Put a lock on the bedroom door—not that you'll be doing anything interesting behind it for some time, but it keeps the kids out.

237 Assuming intimate relations will resume as normal

You'll look back on your efforts to start a family as the halcyon days of your sexual life—not only were intimate relations welcomed, they were actively encouraged, albeit on certain days of the calendar month. The arrival of children would have to be one of nature's great methods of family planning—after they've arrived, the plan seems to be to not risk any future arrivals. This is a time when men need to be understanding—your partner may not be so keen on recreational activities in the bedroom and any suggestion to try them elsewhere will be met with disbelief, especially when you point out that it seems to work in movies of a certain persuasion. Be patient. Express your physical affection in other ways—massage, non-sexual touch or painting the house.

238 Allowing your child to watch too much television

How much is too much? Well, how long is a metre of string? The Australian government (or at least the relevant subsection thereof) recommends no more than two hours of non-educational screen time per day. This includes all computers, video games and television. Many authorities recommend no television at all for babies and toddlers and, when you watch the hypnotic preschool programs that are screened for them, you can understand their point. *Play School* apart, modern programming for the very young encourages them to be about as active as that firmly rooted weed in *Bill and Ben*.

Others, particularly those with degrees in communications and media studies, insist that television does no harm and may be of some benefit, arguing that the complicated plot structures of *Bananas in Pyjamas* encourage lateral thinking and problem solving. But is it likely your children will ever be confronted with the need to find Morgan the Teddy Bear's slippers in a real-life scenario? Can they extrapolate that not all bananas are capable of speech and, yes, it's okay to eat them?

Television is fine in moderation if you actively monitor what the children are watching. Perhaps you could watch their favourite programs with them and have an interesting discussion about why Hannah Montana lives such a seemingly incongruous lifestyle. When your children reach school age, ban all TV in the morning and set an overall limit for screen time during the week. Otherwise, the electronic babysitter, so enthusiastically resorted to by harried parents for a moment's peace when they return from the supermarket, will quickly become the digital tyrant. Once switched on, television becomes ever more difficult to switch off. The threat to remove it altogether rings hollow because the children know full well that you'll be glued to it, stiff drink in hand, as soon as they've gone to bed.

CONCLUSION

'I figure that if the children are alive when I get home,
I've done my job.'
Roseanne Barr

This page can be used as a reflection of your empty life.

When parenthood is getting me down, my father likes to quote the opening line of a poem by Arthur Hugh Clough:

Say not the struggle naught availeth!

In other words, don't believe that nothing is coming from your hard work—you are making progress, however unrecognisable and incremental that progress may be. Unfortunately, this is the poem that Oklahoma City bomber Timothy McVeigh chose to be read out at his execution, but apart from that, the sentiment is a good one for parents to remember in time of self-doubt. My father's other favourite—he's got plenty of 'em—is: 'This too shall pass'. As, indeed, did Timothy McVeigh, somewhat hastily.

However, they are two planks of comfort to cling to: you *are* making a difference and everything in life, good or ill, is only for now. It's all just a phase and your children grow and move away from you so quickly. But enjoy the journey, surrender to the chaos and let your children teach you as much as you teach them.

CONCLUSION

So while we're in the mood for nauseating platitudes, I'm going to leave you with a platitude of my own, a talisman, if you will, to guide you through your parenting journey. One simple acronym that tells you all you need to give your child. It doesn't tell you how to achieve it—I'd be getting the Nobel Prize if I could figure that out—but it's a useful starting point.

PLENTY

P is for Protection
   L is for Love
      E is for Education
         N is for Nourishment
           T is for Trust
              Y is for Yoyo

Yes, it does kind of peter out towards the end but, come on—they've got to have something to play with. If you can give your child PLENTY, you have done your job as a parent. How much PLENTY does one have to give? Therein lies the dilemma. Funny as it seems, I suspect we're giving them too much. Not that they don't deserve it, but if we give it to them too readily, they're less likely to go out and earn it for themselves. As Goethe said a couple of centuries ago:

> Too many parents make life hard for their children by trying, too zealously, to make it easy for them.

Conclusion

In the end, the most important thing you can teach your child is a lesson many parents are reluctant to impart: it is teaching your children how to get along without you.

APPENDIX
(LARGELY USELESS ORGAN BUT DOUBTLESS ONE CHILD WILL NEED IT REMOVED)

Sometimes in your quest for a better understanding of your relationship with your children, it's handy to go to the source. You'd be surprised what your children can teach you about your own behaviour—unpleasantly surprised, usually. So I asked my children to write down ten bad habits of their ineffective parents or ways they could improve their feeble child-rearing. Here is their sage advice, unedited. At least we've taught them how to spell.

10 Ways in Which Parents Can Improve How They Deal with Their Children

By Charlotte Biggins (Aged 9)

1. Don't make an enormous fuss over something little (For Mum)
2. Don't shout too much
3. Get to know the people at school instead of asking people who they are (For Dad)
4. Stay for morning lines
5. Be kind to us if we can't get to sleep

Appendix

6. Leave us in peace if we are happy (Because we rarely ever are)
7. On our birthday be our personal slaves (You haven't been doing that lately)
8. Learn to Love Sydney
9. Be Patient
10. Play with us more

Not entirely sure where 'Learn to love Sydney' came from, and it's perhaps not a great deal of help if you live in Adelaide or Birmingham, but it's something for us all to reflect on. Somewhat disturbing that a nine-year-old can be so world-weary as to describe herself as rarely happy, but good to see her rounding out with the universal plea of all children: 'Play with us more'. By all means, I'd be happy to—if you can think of something a little more interesting for me to play than Littlest Pet Shop.

How did the other child rate her parents' performance?

10 Bad Habits of My Parents
By Imogen Biggins (Aged 9)

1. They shout too much
2. They get annoyed too easily
3. They forget about pocket money
4. They spend too much time on the computer

APPENDIX

5. They don't always understand
6. They never let you finish your sentence
7. They confuse you (usually with schoolwork)
8. They swear (sometimes)
9. They talk to other parents too often
10. They don't let you invite many friends over

BONUS

11. They get worried
12. They make things sound as if it's your fault
13. They nag you

An extra three examples of our failings—even for a twin she's never one to do things by halves. Still, on a brighter note, this list was dedicated to 'DAD, The BEST of all DADS'—so God knows what that says about the rest of you.